IMAGES OF ENGLAND

CENTRAL BIRMINGHAM PUBS
VOLUME II

IMAGES OF ENGLAND

CENTRAL BIRMINGHAM PUBS

VOLUME II

JOSEPH McKENNA

TEMPUS

First published 2006

Tempus Publishing Limited
The Mill, Brimscombe Port,
Stroud, Gloucestershire, GL5 2QG
www.tempus-publishing.com

British Library Cataloguing in Publication Data.
A catalogue record for this book is available from the British Library.

ISBN 0 7524 4144 2

Typesetting and origination by Tempus Publishing Limited.
Printed in Great Britain.

CONTENTS

ACKNOWLEDGEMENTS

My thanks to Bolt, Yampy, the lad Steve, Tony, Norman and Malc, for their companionship and humour in our perambulations of central Birmingham in the '80s and '90s, in search of the perfect local, and of course a good night out.

INTRODUCTION

This is the third of a series of books on Birmingham pubs, published by Tempus. The first book Birmingham Pubs, was compiled by Keith Turner in 1999. It gave a general overview of the public houses of Birmingham and its suburbs. The second book looked in more detail at the social and historical functions of the public house within the centre of Birmingham, and in particular at those pubs in the Bull Ring and those lying within the Inner Ring Road. This third book continues with a survey of the city's pubs within the Middle Ring Road.

This is the heart of the city, and here are still to be found the factories and forges that made Birmingham the first manufacturing town in the world. To wander through Digbeth, Deritend and Bordesley, is to travel back a hundred years in time. It is an area dominated by factories and warehouses and of course the great railway arches of the old Birmingham and Derby Railway. Below your feet, now culverted in a glorified sewer, and largely unseen, is the river Rea, which once powered the mills that kick-started the Industrial Revolution within the city. Eastside, Cheapside and the Gay Quarter are included, pubs old and new. Holloway Head and up to Five Ways, another little un-explored part of the city centre is included. The edges of Ladywood and the Colmore Estate beyond Great Charles Street and up to St Paul's Square, are surveyed for pubs and beerhouses, some dating back 200 years. Then on to Gosta Green and the Jennens Estate, linking up to the survey of the previous book.

Up to the 1930s the men and women that worked in the factories still lived here, tongue by jowl in the warren of back streets that in some cases have still survived. The people are gone now, moved out under slum clearance schemes, but they left behind them in these largely unexplored part of the city an echo of themselves in the public houses that remain. These are not the big calling houses to be found in the Arcadian Centre or along Broad Street. They are small homely pubs, just off a main road somewhere, still divided up into bars, lounges and smoke rooms. In winter they have coal fires, and serve up fully flavoured winter ales, pulled from original hand pumps. In summer their pub doors are propped open by a bar stool to allow in the sun's warmth, and old men remove their jackets – and even their caps – and chat about long-gone days. Barely a twenty-minute walk from the hustle and bustle of the Bull Ring, they are still to be found. They have a particular, indefinable quality which permeates them. They have an atmosphere – a character, not found in the bistro-bars of Broad Street or Brindley Wharf. These public houses have reached a mellow state of maturity. Their interiors reveal themselves by degrees, little knick-knacks, souvenirs, objects of unfathomable use, are to be seen on the original bar fittings and on every available surface. On a purpose-built shelf in the bar you will more as like see the darts or Sunday League football trophies; items that reveal that these houses are truly locals – part of the working community. Every decade or so, the patina of life – the nicotine-stained walls and ceilings – are decorated in fresh cream paint, the woodwork is freshened up with a coat of brown gloss. It is an occasion that disturbs the regulars, who can't see the need for such disruption to their lives. Change and progress are alien to the customers of public houses here. They have favoured seats, and are visibly put out when they see a stranger sitting in their seat. In other pubs they prefer to stand at the bar. They too have their particular favoured place, and woe-betide you if you stand there. The right to stand in such a place only comes after a long apprenticeship. The pubs of my youth are now largely gone, but comparable gems have survived here somehow, places where I can still call up a pint of mild, and sit and daydream.

It would be arrogant to say that I have included all the pubs that are, or have been, here. I know that I have not, but I have done my best. Beerhouses (pubs with incomplete licenses) were not listed in Kelly's Directories until 1937, and even then there are references to beerhouses without names. Building plans, some dating from the mid-nineteenth century, do not always give the name of the house, which is equally frustrating. Lists of publicans, their dates of arrival and departure, are not given unless there is a point of interest to be gained. Such a list would in itself be penkerishly boring. The main source for this study has been the Trade Directories of Birmingham dating from 1767 to 1974, continued by telephone directories up to the present day. *Aris's Birmingham Gazette*, from 1741, contains a wealth of advertisements and obituaries relating to pubs and publicans. Maps, and in particular the Rating Plans of 1870, show the location of public houses and the lesser beerhouses, while building plans show the changes that have been wrought over the years. Here it should be mentioned that invariably these works were carried out by William Jenkins or the firm of James & Lister Lea. Further research really does need to be done concerning these architects.

ONE

THE HIGH
STREET

ONE

THE HIGH STREET

Digbeth High Street

This progression is like a pub crawl, it staggers across the road and back again, as we make our way down the hill towards Deritend. The house numbering which might confuse, is simple enough. The lower numbers are on the south side of the High Street down to just beyond Rea Street, then crossing over the road to Milk Street increase as we re-climb the hill towards St Martin's parish church. On the other side of the river the numbering starts again. Of course over the 250 years since the street was originally given house numbers, there has been some change. Pubs are therefore given their present numbers if the they still exist, and the number they once possessed if they do not.

Excluding the Royal George, which was included in the previous book on the pubs of the Bull Ring and Inner Ring Road, the next pub, apparently right next door, was the Pavilion, at 143 Digbeth High Street, in business for just one year, 1893, under licensee Alfred Hardy. Barely a step away was the White Hart, formerly at 139 Digbeth High Street. The white hart was the heraldic symbol of King Richard II, and many old public houses with this name date from the third quarter of the fourteenth century. Such seems to be the case with this house. Humphrey Jurdon leased the Whyte Hart, as it was written at the time, and by then an established inn, from the Guild of the Holy Cross during the early sixteenth century. William Hutton, Birmingham's first historian, records that the last visitation of the plague originated from here, brought from London in a parcel of clothes. In the following century the White Hart was used as a meeting place for the blacksmiths of the town, who were then concentrated in the Digbeth Quarter. In 1743 *Aris's Gazette* advertised:

> To be Lett, and entered upon immediately, Five Smith Shops, with a Ware Chamber,
> In the Backside behind the White Hart Inn, in Digbeth Street, Birmingham.

The owner of the White Hart in 1767 was William Colmore, of a junior branch of the land-owning Colmore family of New Hall. During his time, as the trade directories reveal, stagecoaches embarked from here and carriers used the inn as a staging post for transporting

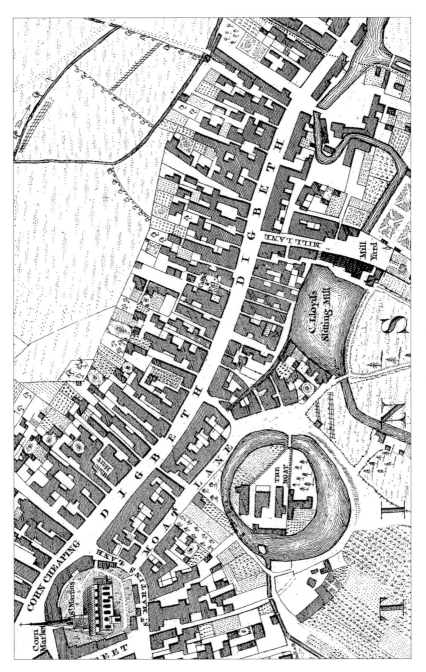

Digbeth, from Bradford's Plan of Birmingham, 1750.

The remains of the war-damaged Talbot, 1956.

goods to London and Cambridge. William Steen was landlord after Colmore, up to 1786. The local barley farmers met at the White Hart in 1791, following an advertisement in the *Gazette* of 3 January, to discuss a new duty levied on malt. Socially, this old house was one-time home to the Musical Society, before its move to the Bell, in Phillips Street. Thomas Marston was landlord in 1800. His widow, Elizabeth, was licensee in 1811. By 1828, under Thomas Bull, the house was described as a 'commercial hotel'. Thomas Brooks was the White Hart's last landlord. It closed apparently in early 1854, was demolished sometime after, and the site was re-developed.

Across the road, and twenty yards or so further down, was the Talbot, at 14 Digbeth High Street. It was a mid to late eighteenth-century public house, with a rear entrance onto Moat Row. Alongside the pub was a passageway that linked the two roads. Joseph Webb was licensee from 1785 to post-1816. He was followed by William Swinburn, and later Joseph Twigg, who was landlord up to 1829. With the opening of Smithfield Wholesale Market in 1881, the main entrance of the Talbot, following some renovation, was changed to 24 Moat Row. In the following decade the pub became a Holt Brewery tied house. There is an advertisement for the Talbot in the *Birmingham Echo* for 11 October 1913:

FRANK RICHARDS, the Talbot Inn, Moat Lane. Late of the Crown and Anchor, Chapel Street. Fully Licensed. Holt Brewery Specialities in grand condition. Catering all day. Frank extends a hearty welcome to all old and new friends.

The Horse & Jockey, 1889.

In 1934 the Talbot became an Ansell's house. It was badly damaged during the Blitz of 1941, its top storeys were removed, and the house was capped off at first-floor level. The Talbot continued in business until 1944, when its license was suspended. Thereafter the Licensing Justices renewed it on an annual basis until 1959. In that year the license was transferred to the proposed Bull Ring Tavern at the junction of St Martin's Lane and Moat Lane. The Talbot was closed, and only after a decade or so was it demolished and the site redeveloped.

Immediately across the road from the Talbot was the old Cold Storage building, whose entrance yard to the right was the site of the King's Head at 127 Digbeth High Street. The earliest verifiable licensee of this pub was Arthur Mathieson in 1827, though it seems probable that the pub was much older. Mathieson was here until 1839, when he was succeeded by Thomas Horton. A number of licensees followed, none of whom stand out until the arrival of the Hungarian, Gutave Niay, who was licensee briefly from 1877 to 1879. The King's Head closed in 1898 for the building of the above Cold Storage, designed by Ernest Bewley and opened in the following year. Three doors down at 124 was the Woolpack, who's sign reminds us that in earlier years Birmingham was an important centre for the wool trade, being strategically placed between the Cotswolds, East Anglia and the north. John Doody was landlord of this house from 1785, up to his death on 18 October 1796. Almost facing, across the road, was the White Swan, at 27 High Street. Edward Wright was its landlord in 1865.

The Rose, on the corner with Allison Street, c. 1890. An important, if damaged, old print.

A little way down the road at the junction of Allison Street, and facing Upper Mill Lane, was the Horse & Jockey. This was a three-storey Georgian house dating from the second half of the eighteenth century. The obituary of licensee, John Oldnall, occurs in the *Birmingham Gazette* for 23 February 1801. He first appears as licensee in the directory of 1785. In 1818, William Tranter, a former gunmaker, is listed as landlord. He died, aged thirty-nine, on Christmas Eve 1827. His successors were Edward and Mary Rogers, who between them were licensees at the Horse & Jockey for forty-nine years, up to 1877. David Bowsher was put in to run the pub until it could be sold. The buyers in the following year were the Trent Brewery of Burton-on-Trent. Alterations were carried out later that year to the designs of Birmingham architect Charles J. Hodson. Later work was undertaken under the guidance of William Jenkins in September 1888. A beer store was added the following year, to a design by Richard Turner. The Horse & Jockey was closed in 1896 and demolished, to be replaced by yard space for the Digbeth Refrigeration Works. The corner site occupied by the Horse & Jockey was later built upon and became the Midland Red Social Club. This was later converted into the present public house on the site, Hennesey's. Situated on the other corner of Allison Street with a large lantern above its corner doorway, the Rose is first listed in the trade directory of 1865. Thomas Hall was credited as licensee then. About 1890 the house was added to the Holt Brewery stable of tied houses. The Rose was demolished in 1909 for the construction of Henry Stilgoe's Digbeth Police Station of 1911. What must have been next door, and also demolished in the name of law and order, was the Clements Vaults at 102. It opened in 1893 with Edward Hope as its first licensee, and closed in 1907.

In that part of the High Street between Upper Mill Lane and Smithfield Street was the old timber-framed Hop Pole at 32 Digbeth High Street. It was in existence, as the directories reveal, between 1767 and 1777, under landlord Paul Field. The probability is that it was much older. Two or three doors down was the Three Tuns, an M&B house. It originated about 1790, and given the possibility of some sort of street renumbering, may in fact be the Hop Pole re-named. Its licensee up to his death in May 1796 was Samuel Thompson. During the stewardship of Thomas Barnes, landlord for a quarter of a century, from 1840 to 1864, the emphasis of the pub shifted from the High Street to Smithfield Street behind. Rather like the Talbot, it appears to have been servicing a market's clientele. Yet despite this shift of emphasis, alterations to the Digbeth frontage were carried out to the drawings of James Yates, for owners, M&B, and licensee, J.W. Barton, from 9 March 1897. Barton remained as licensee up to the outbreak of the First World War, when he was replaced by the Three Tuns' last three licensees, John Baylis, Charles Brown and John Bloom. The Tuns closed in 1937.

Over the road at 109 High Street, on the corner of Meriden Street, was the Castle & Falcon, shown and named on Samuel Bradford's Plan of Birmingham for 1750. Thomas Hammond was licensee from 1786 to 1800. In 1800 its licensee was Hannah Denston. She remained here until 1818. A few years later the building next door was demolished, and Meriden Street was cut alongside, turning the Castle & Falcon into a corner house. Thomas Greensill is listed as licensee in Pigot's 1828 Warwickshire Directory. He was followed by his son, George. Between them the Greensills were landlords of the Castle & Falcon for over forty years. Sometime about 1850 the house was rebuilt in brick. Additions and alterations were carried out from plans drawn-up by architect John Johnson on 9 November 1877, and by builders Surman & Sons in May 1887. Twenty years later, in 1907, architect W.H. Ward undertook further work on the Castle & Falcon, producing the building that we see today, with bands of yellow and blue brick. He gave the house a large semi-circular window, which filled the whole of the High Street frontage. The Castle & Falcon closed in November 1958, and was converted into the Fancy Silk Store (Birmingham) Ltd. Its license was transferred to the Brewery Tavern, Bloomsbury Street.

Facing Smithfield Garage, back in the 1950s, was the Unicorn Inn, at 46 Digbeth High Street. Its date of origin is unknown. By 1767 it was being run by John Davenport, whose descendant, another John Davenport, would later go on to establish the brewery named after them at Bath Row in 1867. Upon John's death his widow took over, running the house until her death in December 1779. Pre-1890 the Unicorn was bought by the Holt Brewery, and its frontage, if not the entire pub, was rebuilt according to plans drawn-up by James & Lister Lea, on 30 May 1891. After one or two other licensees, Edward Jeffreys was appointed landlord in 1899. He remained here for twenty-two years, before retiring in 1922. The license of the Unicorn was suspended in 1944, but thereafter was re-issued on an annual basis up to 1955. The Unicorn closed on 7 February of that year. More or less on the site of the Unicorn is the present-day Dubliner. A 1970s public house, it was

The Three Tuns, an M&B house, 1935.

originally known as the Tollgate. The name was later changed to the Barrel Organ, and the pub became a popular live music venue, with jazz and blues sessions. During the 1990s the house was reinvented as the Dubliner, when Digbeth was designated the Irish Quarter. The Dubliner is getting there, but still lacks the intimacy of more traditional evolved Victorian pubs run by Irish people.

Beneath the footings of Smithfield Garage are the remains of a far more ancient public house, the Board. It is first referred to in a deed of 1518, where the High Bailiff, Roger Foxall, leased a tan yard nearby, on behalf of Edward Bermingham, lord of the manor. Its inn sign was a plain deal board, lacking any information. It was an army billeting house before the building of the barracks, and as such did sometimes present problems to unwary young soldiers, who, having been given orders to notify the landlord of arriving troops, sometimes failed to find it, due to lack of identification. To confuse matters even more, in the directory of 1861 the house is identified as the Naked Board. For much of the nineteenth century the house was used as a wine and spirits store. The Board was closed and converted to other uses, before being demolished for the construction of the Garage. Also lost beneath Smithfield Garage was the Beehive Tavern, at 115 Digbeth High Street. It was a beerhouse, as opposed to a public house, not possessing a full license. Local artist, A. Tarlington, painted a pen and wash picture of the house in 1872, the name, Beehive Tavern, painted on the front of the premises. It was a curious tall, narrow-fronted building, with bow windows either side of a central door. It was three storeys in height, but only had one central window on each of its upper two floors. In 1872, owner, Mrs Ann Carver, was described as a 'beer retailer'.

The Dubliner, in the Irish Quarter.

Right: *Bob Brettle, bare-knuckle boxer and licensee of the White Lion.*

At 95-98 Digbeth High Street was the White Lion, a medieval timber-framed house, probably as old as the Old Crown. It was a low-roofed building with a central pointed gable. Facing on to the street it had six unequal sized and odd-shaped windows. To one side was a gateway leading to the inn yard beyond, wide enough to allow a coach to pass. In the eighteenth century, when timber-framing was considered too provincial, the front of the house was plastered over to give the impression of stone. William Crane is listed as landlord from 1767 to 1777. The White Lion was owned by the Governors of King Edward School in New Street, who leased out the house, as is witnessed in an advertisement in *Aris's Gazette* for 6 February 1797. As with a number of large public houses in the town, soldiers were billeted here. They were provided with accommodation in 'soldiers' rooms' in a building detached from the house proper.

Undoubtedly the most famous licensee here was the prize fighter, Bob Brettle. He was born at Portobello, near Edinburgh, in January 1832, and journeyed down to Birmingham to fight James Malpas for a purse of £50, on 14 February 1854. In November, now based in Birmingham, he fought Jack Jones of Portsmouth for £100. A year later in November 1855 he defeated Roger Coyne of Birmingham, and then Sam Simmonds near Didcot, on 3 June

The White Lion, Digbeth.

1856, for £200, plus side bets. The 'Birmingham Pet' as he was now known, next fought Job Cobley in August 1857, winning in the 47th bloody round. Bob Travers next fell to Brettle, with prize money of £100. Jem Mace of Norwich likewise was defeated on 21 September 1858. Mismatched, Brettle's last fight was against the British champion, Tom Sayers, a formidable fighter. The match took place at Ashford on 20 September 1858. In a hard-fought contest, Brettle managed to knock Sayers down in the second, but in the seventh, failing to connect with a left hook, Sayers countered with a heavy blow to his exposed shoulder, dislocating it in the process. Brettle, in extreme pain, was unable to continue. He had made his money, and retired after the fight to become licensee of the White Lion. As a point of interest, one of Brettle's backers for a number of years was the notorious Dr William Palmer, the Rugely Poisoner. Brettle proved to be the White Lion's last landlord. The house was closed following compulsory purchase in 1869, and demolished for road widening. Brettle died in 1872, and was buried in Harborne churchyard. Following the completion of the works, a new White Lion was built on a smaller scale, but was soon renamed the British Lion. Its licensee from 1879 to 1881, was Michael Fanning. This house likewise was closed, demolished, and lies beneath the present Smithfield Garage.

The Old Guy Inn was situated on the site of the present Midland Red Coach Station. Its original name was the Old Guy of Warwick, taking its name from a semi-mythical character, Guy, Earl of Warwick, who went around doing deeds of valour, and slaying giant cattle. Christopher Fuller was licensee in 1767, according to the town's first trade directory. James Lees had taken over by 1776. During the 1850s the house changed its name to the Albion, after having a brick front added. This was under licensee, Benjamin Jenkins. By 1863, however, it had reverted to its original name under J. Cleton. By the 1870s the house was given a complete overhaul. Landlord Henry Griffiths called in architect Henry Holmes in February 1877 to design a new pub, with large picture windows. At the turn of the century the house was noted for its entertainment in the form of freak shows, featuring Siamese twins, the fat lady and her sister the bearded lady, and any number of dwarfs. It must have been rather akin to the present Broad Street on a Saturday night. The Old Guy's license was withdrawn, and the pub closed in 1933, Albert Rose being its last licensee. Also gone beneath the coach station was the Hand & Glove of 1767 to 1770, under licensee Joseph Latham, and the 1860s Wine & Liquor Vaults, at 71-72 High Street, run by Charles Swingler.

Facing the coach station at 83 Digbeth High Street was the Horse & Groom. In business by 1812, Edward Edwards is listed in the directory of the day as the pub's first landlord. He was a chair-maker by trade, and appears to have opened the house as an investment. His obituary in 1822 appears in the *Birmingham Gazette*. His widow Elizabeth continued in the dual occupation begun by her husband until 1827. She was followed as licensee by Thomas Haywood, and he by William Dipple and George Bennett. Alterations and additions were carried out to this Georgian house based on the plans drawn-up for licensee Lewis Phillip Ashcroft by architect Charles Floyd, on 23 July 1896. Of the Horse & Groom's more notable licensees was Caesar Jenkyns, licensee from 1905 to 1909. Jenkyns was a Welsh International footballer, playing the domestic game for Small Heath FC (later to become Birmingham City). He had a tough uncompromising attitude towards tackling, and what to him was no more than a vigorous shoulder charge, was seen by others as nothing short of GBH. The response to such tackling boosted the sales of the newly invented shin guards. Jenkyns died in 1941 at the Queen Elizabeth Hospital, at the age of seventy-four. In a somewhat generous obituary, the *Evening Despatch* described him as 'one of the best-known figures in the football world of half a century ago…'. Some eight licensees followed Jenkyns at the Horse & Groom, which closed on 30 December 1933, its last licensee, Mrs Gertrude Carr, received a very modest £100 in compensation.

Very briefly in 1865, at 81 Digbeth High Street, was the New Inn, under licensee William Milnes. Immediately next door is one of the oldest public houses in Birmingham, the Old Bull's Head, also known as the Little Bull's Head, in deference to the nearby larger Big Bull's Head. A former M&B house, it was briefly known as the Roscommon Bar, but is now known as the Kerry Man, reflecting its position in the recently designated Irish Quarter of the city. Back at the turn of the twentieth century, when it was still the Bull's Head, it was used by a gang of local toughs known as the 'Epsom Gang'. There is a story told of how one Thomas Larvin, alias Tommy Tank, 'who sold kippers from a pony-drawn cart – a man known to have drunk in everyone of the forty-five pubs within 250 yards of Digbeth Police Station – and to have been banned from everyone of them too', was smuggled into the back room of the Bull by members of the gang. While he was drinking, other members of the gang un-tethered his pony from a lamp post outside, took it up the narrow iron-gated entry at the side of the pub, dismantled his flat-bottomed cart, and carried it sideways up the entry too, where they reassembled it, and re-harnessed the pony. Later that night as Tommy, worse for the drink, left the pub, he discovered that his pony and cart had gone.

The Kerryman, formerly the Old Bull's Head.

As panic set in, he was informed that there was a pony and cart up the entry. Up he went to retrieve them, but how to get them back down in his present state was beyond him.

The earliest known representation of the Bull's Head, a drawing by local artist A. Tarlington in 1870, shows it as a square-built Georgian house of three storeys, with a central door on the ground floor, and a window either side. Above the door was the statue of a bull's head. The front of the pub was rebuilt about 1880, and again a few years after M&B took over the pub on 25 August 1900. The actual work was carried out from plans submitted in November 1905. With some slight variations, it became the pub that we see today. The first known licensee of the Bull's Head was a Mrs Moore, whose obituary appears in *Aris's Gazette*. She died on 4 September 1755. Thomas Picking was here from 1764 to 1768. He was followed by Samuel Reynolds, Thomas Haywood, John Smith and William Humphreys, who saw in the nineteenth century as the pub's landlord. During the time of landlord John Silk (1848-50) the house became the Old Bull's Head. Now lying within the city's Irish Quarter, it was not until 1945 that it gained its first Irish licensee, Noel Malone. At the turn of the twenty-first century it became the Kerry Man. Hopefully one day it will regain its former name of the Old Bull's Head, a name it held for the best part of 250 years.

The Big Bull's Head.

In between the two Bull's Heads was the Gun, at 75 Digbeth High Street. Digbeth was the old Gun Quarter before its move to the Weaman Estate in the mid-eighteenth century. The Gun is a reminder of that trade, which originated during the reign of William III. The Gun's landlord in 1767 was the aptly named Harry Gunn. His widow Ann succeeded him as licensee in 1777.

Built right up against the original bank of the river Rea, the Big Bull's Head was originally known as the Stag & Pheasant in the early part of the nineteenth century. As early as 1518 there was a licensed house on the site. Un-named, it is referred to only by the name of its publican, one Ward. It is mentioned in a Release, where Roger Foxall, the High Bailiff, leased neighbouring land to be used as a tanyard. The Big Bull's Head, so named to differentiate it from the Bull's Head, a few doors away, was rebuilt (possibly for a second or third time) in 1858, with later alterations by Thomas Jabet in 1880; stabling was added in 1885 under Edward Ward, and a redesigned ground floor by William Hale, also in 1885. The Big Bull's Head was bought up by William Jones, who established what we would describe today as a 'pubco'. He renamed the house the Criterion, the company's name. With the collapse of the Criterion Company, Atkinson's of Aston bought the house, which reverted back to its original name in 1926. The pub survives still, nominally an M&B house, whose historical licensing trade site stretches back almost 500 years. On the other side of Milk Street from the Big Bull's Head was the Liquor Vaults, a beerhouse, which along with two adjoining shops were designed by pub architect William Jenkins on 24 November 1882.

The Old Leathern Bottle and Three Crowns, c. 1885.

At 221-222 Digbeth High Street was the Leathern Bottle and the Three Crowns; two public houses existing side by side, built as one timber-framed house around 1625. The Three Crowns did have a date of 'AD 1586' painted above the doorway, suggesting that the house had been rebuilt. In the Georgian era the old building was covered in stucco in an attempt to modernise it and give the impression that it was built of stone. The building lay between two streams that made up the river here, and following the raising up of the roadway, post-1730, the building was left some 3ft below the road. Stout iron railings were erected to prevent pedestrians falling from the pathway above. There is a short death notice in the *Birmingham Gazette* of 12 September 1814 for one-time licensee of the Leathern Bottle, William Rostill Lowe, and a reference to the licensee of the Three Crowns, Thomas Shore, with the death of his son, Samuel, 'who died at his father's home, the Three Crowns, Deritend' on 14 November 1816. The two inns, brought back under common ownership, successively passed to Benjamin Hawkins, John Rhodes, William Knock, Daniel, and later John Ruston, and others, eventually passing into the hands of the Ryland family. During this period the running of the two public houses was left to others, as is evidenced in the trade directories of the town. In 1866 the two houses were bought by John Brearley Payn, who eventually sold them on to George Hemming, their last owner. Alterations were carried out to the Three Crowns, when Albert Noble was licensee, from plans drawn-up by architect J.D. Wood on 11 November 1883. The Leather Bottle, its name slightly changed by this time, and the Three Crowns (a reference to the Three Wise Men), were closed and the building was demolished in 1891-2. The last licensee was Mrs Emily Grimes. The site of these two old public houses is now occupied by the Digbeth annexe of South Birmingham College.

The Three Crowns, Deritend, c. 1889.

Along Digbeth High Street over the years there were six beerhouses, whose locations are not known. There was the Lamp Tavern of 1767, under landlord Henry Coleman, and the Crown & Ball of the same date, run by landlady Elizabeth Bridgens. The Death of General Wolf, most probably abbreviated to the General Wolfe, was an army recruiting house, as is evidenced in an advertisement in the *Gazette* of 2 August 1779, when 'All young men who have spirit and resolution to stand forth in the defence of their country', were asked to apply to Recruiting Sergeant Pring. Then there was the Stag & Pheasant, brought to life with the obituary of its one-time licensee, Joseph Chinn, who died in 1827, at the comparatively early age of thirty-three. Finally at the opening of the twentieth century two brothers, Billy and Charlie Brown, kept the Lion & Lamb and the Golden Cup, respectively. Billy was apparently one of the last Birmingham bare-knuckle boxers.

Deritend High Street

From Floodgate Street it is possible to see the river Rea, that forms the boundary between Digbeth and Deritend. It looks like an open sewer, but in its day, before it was tamed, it was a broad, slow-moving river given to flash floods. Across the road is the Irish Centre, and alongside of it runs a short road called the Stone Yard. At its junction with the High Street was the curiously named Stone & Gravel. It was a beerhouse dating from the 1780s. There is a very brief reference to it in the obituary of its one-time licensee:

Carey, ----- of the Stone & Gravel, died 10th June 1783.
(*Aris's Gazette* 16.6.1783)

Somewhere close by was the George, not to be confused with the George, or Royal George, on the corner of Park Street. It was situated on the far side of the river, and was offered for sale in *Aris's Gazette*:

June 1, 1764. -- To be sold to the best Bidder, at the Dolphin Inn in Birmingham, on Friday the 22nd Day of June Instant, at Five of the Clock in the Afternoon, according to such conditions as shall then be produced, A Good Substantial Freehold Dwelling House with a Back Kitchen, and Chamber over the same, a Brewhouse, Stabling for five Horses, and a good Garden thereto belonging, situate at the Top of Deritend near Birmingham aforesaid, for several years past 'til lately used as a Public House, and known as the Sign of the George, and now in the possession of Mrs Sarah Hawkes, Widow.

For further particulars enquire of Mr Hallen, Attorney, Birmingham.

There is an old inn with a swinging sign board, clearly shown on William Westley's Plan of Birmingham for 1731, situated at the crossing over the Rea. Much care was taken in the engraving of such a minute matter. The signboard clearly shows the usual representation of a wool pack, resembling a thick inverted letter 'U'. This would suggest that the public house was either called the Fleece, or more likely the Woolpack. The matter was discussed at some length in Local Notes & Queries No. 125, but with no firm conclusion. On more surer ground was the Ring of Bells, at 8 Deritend High Street. George Wright was its first known licensee. He is listed as landlord from pre-1780 to 1791. In the directory of 1785 the address is given as Deritend Bridge. Richard Hancox, formerly a licensee in Church Street, took over in 1791. He died in December 1797, leaving his widow Ann to run the house until post-1803. Across the road at 223 High Street was the curiously named Measure, a very short-lived house open from 1854-56 under licensee Henry Baker.

At 22 High Street was the Nelson Inn, also known as the Lord Nelson and the Nelson's Head. This public house was situated next door to the more famous Golden Lion, now rebuilt in Cannon Hill Park. The Nelson was a substantial square-built Georgian house of three storeys, with a central doorway and bow windows either side. Its long-term licensee, Thomas Upton, died on 5 April 1828, aged eighty-two. Less than a week later his widow, Jane, died at the age of eighty-one. In 1878 William Evans took over. Two years later alterations and an update to the house were carried out to the designs of the architectural firm of Thompson & Son. In 1890 the Nelson was compulsorily purchased by the City Council and demolished for road widening. The Golden Lion, once believed to have been the house of the Guild of St John, Deritend, but a theory now discredited, was built around 1600.

In the Hearth Tax returns of 1663, William Billingsley is listed as licensee of this three-gabled timber-framed house. In 1738 the house was divided up into six small houses, one of which was called the Star Inn, afterwards renamed the Golden Lion. From 1767 to 1777, Edward Moore was landlord of the Golden Lion. Its address was then given for the first time as 24 High Street, Deritend. Richard Moore, presumably a son, was licensee in 1780. In 1840 Henry Bradshaw became landlord. He and his wife Mary Ann and son Henry ran the Golden Lion for near fifty years. The house became a Beard's Brewery tied house in 1887, with Eliza Robbins as licensee. As with the Nelson, the house was acquired for demolition under a road-widening scheme, but following a successful conservation appeal it was carefully taken down and re-erected in the park. There has been some talk of returning the Golden Lion to a new site in Deritend, but so far nothing has been done.

Across the road from the Golden Lion was the Red Lion, at 199 High Street, Deritend. It was in existence by 1743, as is evidenced by its sale on 19 December of that year. Thomas Cooper was the licensee then, Thomas Warren its owner. In a sale of 1886, the property is listed in some detail. It comprised a:

> ...fully licensed Public House, containing front Bar, Bar Parlour, Wine and Beer Cellars, Four Bedrooms, Club Room, Kitchen, and Brewhouse, let to Mr. John Sergeant.

Opposite above: *The Golden Lion, Deritend, and next door, the Nelson Inn.*

Opposite below: *The rebuilt Golden Lion in Canon Hill Park, 1936.*

Below: *The Old Crown, High Street, Deritend, 1890.*

By direction of the Trustees of the late
A. TOULMIN SMITH.

Sale by Auction of the

FREEHOLD FULLY-LICENSED

CORNER PUBLIC HOUSE,

KNOWN AS

"The Old Crown Inn,"

No. 188 HIGH STREET, DERITEND ;

Freehold Retail Shops & Premises

KNOWN AS

"The Old Crown House,"

Nos. 185½, 186 and 187 HIGH STREET,
DERITEND ; and

Three Freehold Ground Rents.

HIGH STREET and HEATH MILL LANE,
DERITEND.

Fleetwood, Deakin, Hendriks & Co.

are instructed to Sell by Auction, at

The Grand Hotel, Colmore Row, Birmingham,

on

TUESDAY AFTERNOON, MARCH 17th, 1925,

at FOUR o'clock,

subject to conditions to be then produced.

VENDORS' SOLICITORS:—Messrs. RYLAND, MARTINEAU
& CO., 7 Cannon Street, Birmingham

Cards to View from AUCTIONEERS' OFFICES, 29 Newhall
Street, Birmingham. (Telephone: Central 4046 and 4047).

Above left: *The cellar of the Old Crown, 1929.*

Above right: *Sales notice for the Old Crown, 1925.*

In January 1907 the house was sold for £6,900 to next-door neighbours Birds, makers of the well-known custard powder. They demolished it for the building of a new factory.

Five doors down from the previously mentioned Golden Lion was the Nag's Head. It first appears in the trade directory of 1828 with William Huskins listed as landlord. Architect Joseph Frakin undertook alterations and updating to the pub in 1878 for new licensee Francis Nicholson. The license to the Nag's Head was surrendered in 1907 for road widening. In an earlier road-widening scheme the Old Crown was narrowly saved from demolition. In 1868, faced with its imminent demolition, its then owner, Joshua Toulmin Smith, assembled together a rag bag collection of deeds and documents purporting to show that this old timber-framed house had been built in 1368 — exactly 500 years before. It fooled the Council, and the Old Crown was reprieved. The house as we see it today is essentially early sixteenth century, but a recent survey has revealed that it probably dates from 1480. The earliest authentic deed relating to the house as an inn is dated 1589, when Richard Smalbroke of Yardley sold the property to John Dixon, alias Bayles. The licensee at the time was John Hayberd. In 1673 the Dixon family leased the Crown to Edward Barbar, a goldsmith, for a period of twelve years. It was not until the obituary notice of John Hawkes, in August 1789, that the house is referred to as the Old Crown. On 17 March 1925, the Holt Brewery Company acquired the pub at auction. In 1934 when they were taken over, the Old Crown became an Ansell's tied house. In 1976, to the shame of the city, the Planning Committee gave Ansell's permission to gut the interior of the Old Crown. Through the 1980s and early 1990s the house fell into the doldrums, and was closed. It was in want of serious structural repair. A sum in excess of £300,000 was spent repairing and refurbishing it and the Old Crown has re-opened as a free house.

Six doors down from the Old Crown was the Old Fighting Cocks, at 182 High Street. It was an old Georgian house, dating from 1770, under licensee Thomas Crisp. It was de-licensed in the early twentieth century and converted into two shops. Very close by was the Wine Vaults of 1855 under Joseph Tew. Immediately across the road from it was the Green Man at 41 Deritend High Street. The house is not named in the directories until 1818, though its landlady then was in business here as early as 1804. William Bott and his son, William Charles Bott, ran the house for over fifty years between them. In 1914 the Green Man became an M&B tied house. It closed fourteen years later in 1928, Ben Nash was its last licensee. At No. 50 was the Compasses, a beerhouse. There is an advertisement in the *Birmingham Echo* of 11 October 1913, relating to it:

BOB DAVIES, the Compasses, Deritend. For many years at the Old Crown, is mine host of the above house. Newly renovated, painted and upholstered throughout. Fine Club Room free to all approved societies. Headquarters of the Crown Football Club. Holders Noted Midland Ales. B.B., Guinness and Bass, Proprietary Wines, Spirits and Cigars. A call on Bob and his wife will be appreciated.

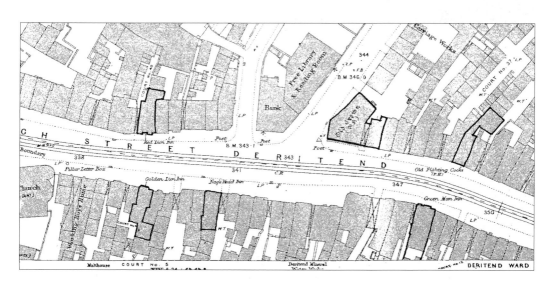

A plan of Deritend High Street, 1887.

At 53 High Street was the Swan with Two Necks, dating from post-1818 under licensee Tom Horn. He was there until 1833. At one time it was briefly known as the Swan Vaults. In 1889 outbuildings were added to the designs of architect E.A. Eaves. The license to the Swan was surrendered to the Justices in January 1907, at the time when the High Street was widened. From 1767 to 1774, Richard Hawkes is listed as licensee of the Barley Mow, at 67 High Street. There is an obituary for a 'Mrs Grange of Sutton, formerly of the Barley Mow, Deritend,' in the 28 December 1795 edition of the *Gazette*.

There are a further four pubs of uncertain location in Deritend: the Windmill, undoubtedly named after Cooper's windmill, off Heath Mill Lane, probably gives a clue to its location; the Rose, run by Joseph Chamberlain in 1767, the Castle, of similar date, under Thomas Gallard, and the Bear. This house was run by Mark Ensor, listed in the directory of 1787. Two years later there is an obituary for relative Luke Ensor, described as 'Master of the Bear, Deritend', (*Aris's Gazette* 21 Dec. 1789).

Bordesley High Street

A few doors up from the junction with Alcester Street, the King's Head was in existence by 1663, where William Pearsall is listed as occupier in the Hearth Tax returns. The house was considerably updated in 1883 to plans drawn-up by Birmingham architect Thomas Jabet, and offered for sale four years later. At the time the licensee was a Mrs Linfoot, and the

Lot 5. BORDESLEY. A Valuable and Important PROPERTY, situate in the best business part of High Street, Bordesley, opposite the end of Adderley Street, and near to Alcester Street, comprising (a)

THE "KING'S HEAD" SPIRIT VAULTS,

with handsome modern front, and with commodious well-arranged Premises, specially adapted for the modern requirements of trade, considered worth a rent of £100 per annum, and now in occupation of Mrs. Linfoot, who will arrange to give early possession to the purchaser. (b) Two handsome Retail SHOPS, with modern plate-glass fronts, being Nos. 58 and 59, in High Street, adjoining, let to Mr. Webb, saddler, and Mr. Kent, hairdresser (on lease), at rents of £30 and £28 respectively. (c) Eleven substantial and handsome HOUSES, known as "Alcester Terrace," lying in the rear of the above, and running through to Alcester Street, all well let, at rents amounting to £157 6s. per annum. The total annual rental, as above, is £315 6s., and the Property is Leasehold for about ninety-four years, at a ground rent of £130. The King's Head is a substantial erection, recently built in the best modern style, and most conveniently arranged, and it occupies a fine business position in a leading thoroughfare. As possession will be given to the purchaser, the sale is especially well worth the attention of brewers. The Retail Shops and other Houses are also of substantial modern erection, and command good tenants.

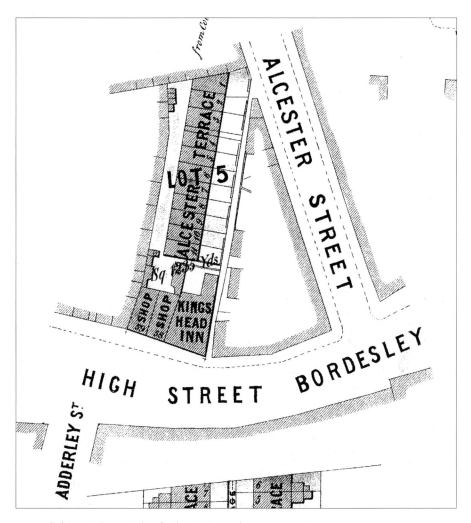

Top and above: *Sales particulars for the King's Head, 25 January 1887.*

Opposite: *The Rainbow, High Street, Bordesley.*

The White Lion, High Street, Bordesley, viewed from the former Camp Hill flyover.

recommended rent was £100 per annum. With a nod towards the new tied house system, the sales catalogue pointed out, 'as possession will be given to the purchaser, the sale is especially well worth the attention of brewers.' The King's Head surrendered its license to the Justices in January 1907. Then licensee, John Harper, was paid £243 in compensation. Across the road is the Rainbow, at 160 High Street, Bordesley. It is an eighteenth-century house in origin, dating back to 1767, when William Lawrence was landlord. He remained there until 1777. During the early nineteenth century the house was known as the Coach & Horses, but had reverted to its original name by 1822. The present house is mid-Victorian in date, believed to have been rebuilt at ground-floor level about 1875-80. A former Atkinson's pub, taken over by M&B, it is now a free house. Of particular interest in its early days of independence was its ever-changing mural on the Adderley Street frontage. As at the start of the twenty-first century its exterior is now painted a rich plum colour.

The White Lion at 144 Bordesley High Street was an old Georgian house, whose first authenticated licensee was Thomas Rogers, who died in November 1828. In November

The former Coach & Horses,
Bordesley, 1986.

1882, William Jenkins drew-up plans for the updating of the house. Taken over by Ansells, James & Lister Lea were called in to design a new house on the site, which opened in 1906. In a breakaway from their recognised terracotta and red brick, they opted for red brick and faience (a creamy-coloured earthenware). The house was closed down in 1974 for road widening and redevelopment near this junction with the Coventry Road.

The Lamp, at 133-134 High Street, was an old Holder's house taken over by M&B. In origin the house dated back to 1701, and was owned by William Brownell, son-in-law of William Tart, who kept the prison next door. Brownell supplied the prisoners with beer. It was not until 1829 that the house was recorded in the directory by name. Taken over by brewers, Holders, in 1891, it was they who rebuilt the house that is seen in the accompanying photograph. The Lamp closed on 31 July 1974 and was demolished for street improvements. The Coach & Horses at 124-5 High Street, Bordesley, was opened in 1827 by William Felton. The Wilkes family, Edwin, wife Emma, son Edwin jr and his wife Ellen, ran the pub for over thirty-five years, from 1852 to 1884.

The Lamp Tavern, Bordesley, from the former Camp Hill flyover, 1965.

In 1936, as part of the 'fewer but better' scheme of the Council, the license was withdrawn, and the premises became offices. Like the above, it was cleared in 1974 for street widening. Three pubs remaining, all of which have now gone, the Castle & Ball of 1818, under landlord, William Felton, the Britannia at No, 72, with Abraham Lowe as licensee in 1855, and the Two Brewers, under William Podmore, 1817-18.

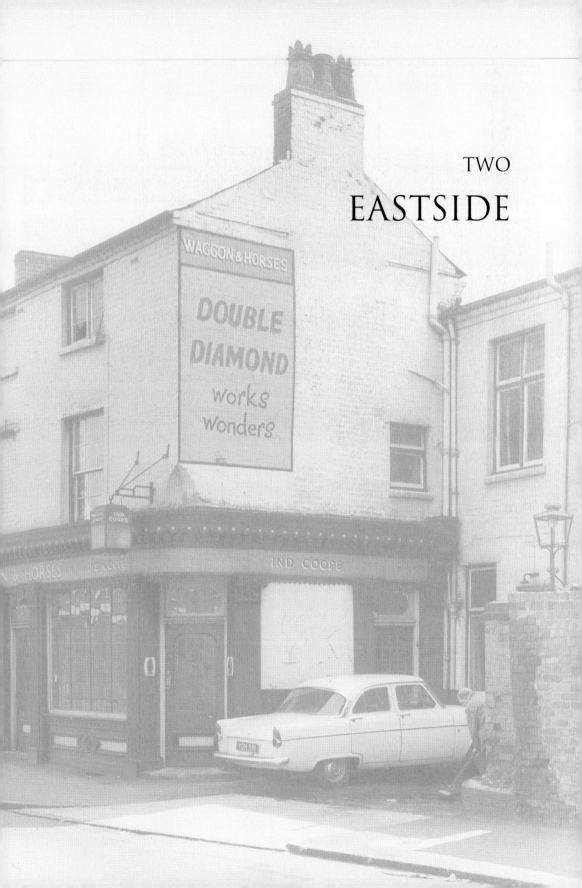

TWO

EASTSIDE

TWO

EASTSIDE

Eastside is the modern name given by the city planners to Digbeth, Deritend and Bordesley, just off the High Street. Leading off from the Bull Ring is Park Street. At No. 3 was the Phoenix, an early nineteenth-century three-storey brick-built house which replaced a former tavern dating back to 1720. There was little adornment to the house save a large lantern over the central doorway, topped by a phoenix rising from the flames. At the heart of the old Irish Quarter, the house was damaged during the anti-Roman Catholic Murphy Riot of 1867, but was repaired. In the late nineteenth century it became an Atkinson's and later an M&B tied house. It closed on 5 August 1965 for the redevelopment of the Bull Ring area. The Daniel O'Connell, at 9 Park Street, was named after Irish MP Daniel O'Connell (1775-1847), who was instrumental in forcing through the Catholic Emancipation Act of 1829. He also advocated Irish Home Rule. The house was a licensed victuallers, situated in the 1860s Irish Quarter. Tom Corbett was licensee in 1862.

The Fox & Grapes is situated on the corner of 16 Freeman Street. It is a two-and-a-half-storey Victorian brick building wrapped around an original late seventeenth or early eighteenth-century building. The house is shown on William Westley's Plan of Birmingham for 1731. It has an attractive carved wooden bar, reputedly destined for the nearby Woodman, but somehow 'mislaid' and installed in the Fox & Grapes. On its panels are rural scenes, and five little woodcutters are carved in relief on its uprights. The house was originally known as the Fox, but nothing is known of its early landlords. Its earliest authenticated licensee was Thomas Benton in 1800. The house became the Fox & Grapes under John Aspinall, landlord during the 1850s. The building was altered in the 1860s, and updated by then brewery owners, Smiths of Aston, in 1925-26. Now a free house, it is the second oldest pub, after the Old Crown, in the city centre. A little further along Freeman Street was the Hogue Inn, a beerhouse, updated by William Jenkins from his plans of 29 August 1876.

The Duke of Cumberland is named after the English commander at the victory over the Scots at Culloden, in 1746. The owner of the Duke in 1812 was William Eades, a horse dealer. This pub never did become a tied house. In 1910 its then owner, Frederick Baker, converted it into a presswork factory. Most of the building was demolished in 1988, and the site was cleared completely for the building of the Millennium Bull Ring Centre. At 37 was

The Fox & Grapes, Freeman Street.

the Red Lion. Thomas Corfield was licensee from 1823 to 1830. John Irons followed. He was licensee up to the pub's closure in 1837. The Anchor was at 46 Park Street, and dated from around 1825. Its first known licensee was Robert Wheeldon, who was followed from 1835 by father and son Henry and Isaac Kirby. They were here up until the late 1850s. At 84 was Chequers, dating from 1767 with Mary Jones as landlady. It was a licensed victuallers, updated in 1890 when Arthur Williams was licensee, from drawings prepared by William Luke Dennis in March of that year. Chequers closed in 1905, George Blakemore being its last landlord.

There were a few un-numbered beerhouses in Park Street. The Lamp under Andrew Murcott, the Flour Basket under John Griffiths, The White Lion under John Deval and James Bayley, and the Vine, later the Old Vine, under Thomas Newey, and later Thomas Glascot, all dated from 1767. The Malt Shovel, apparently a beerhouse, appears in the obituary of Mrs W. Toney in the *Gazette* of 22 November 1802.

Hennesey's, as previously mentioned, is on the corner of Allison Street and High Street. Previously in Allison Street was the White Swan, a beerhouse, at No. 79. Also now gone under a late nineteenth-century improvement scheme was the White Horse on the corner of Bordesley Street. The King's Head dated from 1823 under licensee William Fisher. It closed in 1908, when its lease fell due. John Newey was the last licensee.

A little further down, leading off the High Street, is Meriden Street. On the corner of Bordesley Street is the Spotted Dog. It was originally known as the Dog. It is an early nineteenth century, three-storey converted house. Its first directory-accredited licensee

The Spotted Dog, Meriden Street.

was Thomas Barns in 1812. He was followed by his son, Samuel, who was a maltster by trade. The Spotted Dog was taken over by Atkinson's of Aston, and became a tied house. They engaged architect Francis Bristow to draw up plans on 5 December 1895 for its modernisation, which was carried out in the following year. Atkinsons were taken over in 1959, the pub became an M&B house. Above the present Meriden Street frontage is a rather splendid inn sign depicting a Dalmatian dog at full stretch. Also in Meriden Street, but now gone, was a beerhouse known as the Lion & Dragon. It was a Rushton's tied house, later taken over by Ansells. Additions were made to the pub from plans drawn-up on 31 October 1899, by architect Francis Bristow.

Oxford Street was cut in the late eighteenth century. The earliest known house here was the Crown, dating from 1797. John Jennens was landlord of this beerhouse up to his death in March of that year. A short way off was the Acorn, of 1808, when John Tolley was landlord. It closed in 1877. The trade directory of 1835 lists a pub called the Malt Shovel, in Oxford Street. This appears to be an error for Coventry Street. The Navigation at 44 Oxford Street was on the corner with Bordesley Street and faced the nearby canal wharf. James & Lister Lea carried out updates to the pub in 1881. The Navigation closed in 1958, its license was transferred to the Wellington in Hick Street. The only public house in Oxford Street now is the Old Wharf at No. 21. It opened around 1807 under licensee John Tolley. In December 1889, then landlord Samuel Teague called in the firm of James & Lister Lea to update the house. Some five years later the house was put up for sale by auction and was acquired by Davenports. In a lease-hold agreement, the Old Wharf later became an Ansell's tied house before being sold to Bank's of Wolverhampton, its current owners.

The Old Wharf, 1987.

Along the curiously named Milk Street there were three public houses. The Star, at No. 1, was on the corner of the High Street. The first verifiable licensee was Elizabeth Cole in 1828. Henry Holyoak bought the house in 1834, remaining here until 1861. The Star closed in 1867 and was demolished in the following year. The Old Crown (not to be confused with the more famous house along the High Street) was at 20 Milk Street. It dated from the early 1820s under James Watts. His widow, Elizabeth, took over in 1827. The house, then run by George James, closed in 1842. At 30 Milk Street was the Grapes, listed only in the directory of 1865, with Thomas Ward as licensee. Linking Milk Street to Floodgate Street is a short thoroughfare known as Moores Row. It is situated to the rear of the newly constructed South Birmingham College annexe. Here at 4–5 Moores Row was situated the King's Arms, a two-and-a-half-storey Georgian house with attic windows in the roof space. The Widow Stephens is listed as landlady in the Birmingham trade directory of 1780. She was the wife of Edward Stephens, licensee from 1769 to post-1774. The directories and *Gazette* obituaries list the licensees over the following century up to it closure in 1887. Mrs Emma Flavell was its last licensee.

The King's Arms, Moores Row.

In Floodgate Street was the New Spring Gardens, at Nos 14-15. It was established as a public house by 1828, under landlord William Gibson. In 1901 the name was altered slightly to the Spring Gardens. It closed a decade later, under the 'fewer but better' scheme. John Walter Phillips being its last landlord. There was a beerhouse nearby called the Swan. It opened in 1864, according to Jones' Trade Directory of Birmingham. Joseph Allen was landlord. Thereafter there are no further directory entries. At 72 Floodgate Street was the Rollers' Arms, a reference to the nearby metal rolling mills of Digbeth. The house came into being in 1867, under Joseph Davis. Alterations were carried out to the house from plans drawn-up by pub architects James & Lister Lea on 11 November 1889. In one of its periodic purges the house was closed by the Justices. Closed in 1934 was the beerhouse known as the Floodgate Tavern. Still surviving is the White Swan, known today as Horan's Tavern, on the corner of 92 Floodgate Street and Little Ann Street. It began life in the Victorian era as a beerhouse, gaining a full license in 1887 under licensee Henry Truman. An old Ansell's house, it still sells probably the best mild in Digbeth. A pub to seek out. At 16 Little Ann Street was the Woodman which dated from 1821 under licensee Thomas Hill. It surrendered

Horan's Tavern, formerly the White Swan.

its license in January 1907. Down the far end of Little Ann Street is Bordesley Street. At No. 27 was the Brewer's Arms, an 1820s public house who's first licensee was William Blundell. This was to be another James & Lister Lea makeover pub. William Bedford called in the firm in August 1886. The house closed on 30 December 1933. Alternative pub architect, William Jenkins, drew-up plans on 2 February 1897 to update the White Swan, a beerhouse on the corner of Bordesley Street and Pickford Street. There is now a large factory on the site. The King's Arms was at 45 Bordesley Street, between Oxford Street and Trent Street. It originated in 1853, Harry Allcock was its first landlord. The license to the house was surrendered in January 1907. On the corner of Bordesley Street and 51 New Bartholomew Street was the Mogul. Edward Thompson was landlord from 1812 until his death in April 1814. He took over from his father, William, who had been licensee from 1795. Lesser-known pub architect, William Henry Price, redesigned the house in January 1877, adding a malt house to the rear. The Mogul closed on 30 December 1933.

At the other end of Bartholomew Street, facing the church of the same name, was the Turk's Head, at No. 1. Its licensee from 1797 to 1818 was William Thompson. At 21 Bartholomew Street was the Hen & Chickens, of 1812 to 1818, under licensee Henry Barns. The pub does not appear to have become a tied house. It closed in 1904, John Gibb being its last landlord. The Waggon & Horses was at No. 61. A Victorian beerhouse, it is first registered in the trade directory of 1934 when apparently licensee Edward Burke purchased a full license. The house closed in 1943. Closing exactly one hundred years before was the Noah's Ark at 76 Bartholomew Street. It opened in 1798 under John Dale, landlord until 1820. He was followed by his widow, and she by Richard and his son, Benjamin Palmer.

In New Canal Street, which links Bordesley Street and Fazeley Street, was the Star & Garter at No. 58. It dated from around 1835 and closed during the 1850s. The American Inn, at 71 New Canal Street, was a fairly substantial public house facing Curzon Street Station. It is first listed in 1847, under William Vaughan. It had closed by 1897, Fred Wardle being its last recorded licensee. Also facing the old station, on the corner of New Canal Street and Albert Street, is the Woodman. The pub was designed by the Birmingham architectural firm of James & Lister Lea for Ansell's Brewery, in 1897. The pub is a typical Lea house, constructed in a mixture of red brick and terracotta, with large arched windows. Its exterior is more than matched by its Minton-tiled interior. The smoke room still has its draught screens and the remains of the bell pushes for waiter service. The public bar is likewise tiled, and still retains its original bar back, with round-headed panels of mirror glass, framed in marble wood. The house has a chilling notoriety. Twice a week the Yorkshire Ripper, Peter Sutcliffe, who is serving life for the murder of thirteen women, used to pop into the smoke room to meet up with his lorry driver mates. He used to sit at the white vinyl bench in the corner. During the 1990s the Woodman was statutorily Grade II listed. Bought by the City Council when it was acquiring land for the redevelopment of Eastside, the house, temporarily without a licensee, was broken into and various items were stolen.

Above: *The old smoke room of the Eagle & Tun, Banbury Street, c. 1964.*

Opposite: *The Woodman, New Canal Street, 1975.*

Situated on the corner of New Bartholomew Street was the Hope & Anchor, at 101 New Canal Street. Opened in 1820, it narrowly survived the coming of the railways, when the viaduct was built very close nearby. The house closed when Mrs Florence Allen was landlady, in 1957. There were at least three beerhouses here; the Malt Shovel, closed under the Improvement Scheme, the Skinners Arms, which became a full pub in 1888, under William Wilkins, and which closed in 1924, and the Proof House Tavern, close to the Gun Barrel Proof House, which was closed in December 1933. Just off New Canal Street is Banbury Street. At No. 12 is the Eagle & Tun, designed by James & Lister Lea in 1900 for M&B. It was built on the site of an earlier house of the same name, which dated back to 1834. The pub was briefly renamed the Cauliflower Ear during the 1980s and '90s, and featured on the album cover of UB40's 'Greatest Hits' as well as their follow up, 'UB40 the best of volume two'. Visitors, allegedly, came from as far away as Japan to visit the pub (or so the landlord said). Very sensibly the pub has now reverted back to its original name.

On the corner of Lower Fazeley Street and Heath Mill Lane is the Forge Tavern. In the dark days of the Ansells/M&B duopoly, when there was little choice, the Forge was an oasis in that it sold Marston's. There were two other pubs in Fazeley Street, both of which have now closed. The Vulcan Inn was at No. 20. Thomas Parkes was its earliest landlord, in 1835. William Jenkins updated the pub from his plans of 26 November 1880. With the dispersal of the local population in a slum clearance scheme, the Vulcan surrendered its license in 1933. A year later, on 24 February 1934, the Royal Oak at 86 Fazeley Street also closed.

The Forge Tavern, Fazeley Street, 1957.

This pub, on the corner with Andover Street, dated from 1827; Job Reeves was its licensee. In 1895 it became a Holt's tied house, and underwent updating to the plans of Edward Giles, including the inclusion of a urinal. Further alterations were carried out in 1896. An advertisement of 1913 revealed that the pub consisted of 'roomy bars, good smoke room, large club rooms and an excellent dining room'. The site of the Royal Oak is now occupied by factory offices.

In the Deritend and Bordesley sections of Eastside, there was a little beerhouse called the Beehive, in Allcock Street, brought to our attention with its closure on 31 December 1935. At 19 Allcock Street, on the corner with Adderley Street, was the Great Western, established in 1854. It was taken over by Davenport's Brewery, and featured in their house magazine, *Malt & Hops*, in October 1948. The site of this pub is now occupied by an engineering company. In Adderley Street, at No. 28, is the Waggon & Horses, which originated post-1839 under John Muddyman. Extensive alterations and updating to the house were undertaken from plans drawn-up by William Jenkins in October 1878. Further work was done under the direction of architect Henry Naden a decade later. The Waggon & Horses became an Ansell's tied house, but was sold by them in 1986, following the Monopolies investigation. The new owners, who ran a jazz club, renamed it the Cannonball, taking its name from a jazz musician, Cannonball Adderley. Of late however the old pub has returned to its original name. At 83 Adderley Street was the Adderley Arms, opened in 1859. A new brew-house was added to the pub in 1887, from plans drawn-up by William J.P. Riley. The Adderley Arms closed in 1942, following war-time shortages.

The former Vulcan Inn, Barn Street.

The Waggon & Horses,
Adderley Street, 1967.

The Leicester Arms was at 100 Coventry Street, and dated from around 1827. Its landlord was John Gilbert, there until 1834. With his departure the house was renamed the Dolphin by new owner Joseph Smith. Architect William Wykes was called in to update the pub in November 1884. Following the slum clearances of the 1930s, the Dolphin, under Harry Evans, was closed in 1932 and became a café. At 111 Coventry Street was the Bricklayers Arms, opened in 1858. The house, on the corner of Allison Street, closed in 1870 and was converted into two shops. The Malt Shovel, an old Kelsey's tied house, on the corner of 58 Coventry Street and Milk Street, was first licensed in 1824. In 1877 William Jenkins updated the house for the brewery, which was later taken over by Ansells. Very much a lunch-time pub, drawing its trade from the factory workers, by 1984 trade had slumped so much that the house was closed down. It lay vacant for a couple of years before re-opening as a free house, Billy's. By the summer of 2005 it had closed yet again, awaiting new owners.

Alongside the Old Crown runs Heath Mill Lane, and beyond it is Gibb Street. At 49 Heath Mill Lane was the Pool Tavern, offered for sale on 25 May 1881, with fourteen years remaining on its lease. At 20 Gibb Street was the Fruiterers Arms, dating from 1855; it was run

The former Malt Shovel, Coventry Street.

by George Muddyman and his wife Eliza up to 1871. The house closed in 1916. Great Barr Street is the continuation of Heath Mill Lane. At 71 was the Globe, situated on the corner of Ivy Lane. It came into being around 1853. Henry Hornblower was licensee here for over thirty-six years, from 1860. The house closed in 1940, Alan Lilly being its last licensee. At 99 Great Barr Street was the King's Arms, Joseph Brownell being licensee from 1818 until his death in November 1838. It became an Ansells house, but was forced to close during the 1970s for the cutting of the Middle Ring Road. At 114-115 Great Barr Street was the Minerva. John Bury was licensee when it opened in 1855. The Minerva Vaults, as it became, closed in 1965. Around the corner in Montague Street was the Noah's Ark, originating in 1861, at No. 28. William Jenkins updated the house from his plans of 13 January 1896. The Ark closed in 1972. Leading off from Heath Mill Lane is Liverpool Street. There was a licensed victuallers here, the Malt Shovel, in 1862 under licensee, William Hayes. Also along here, on the corner of Adderley Street, was the nineteenth-century beerhouse, the Albion. In Glover Street, that links Adderley Street and Montague Street, was the Vulcan, at No. 77. It was in business from 1867 to 1926, when its license was transferred to a pub on one of the new Acocks Green council estates. Palmer Street is off Glover Street. There was a Victorian beerhouse here called the Malt Shovel. It appears in the trade directories for the first time in 1940, when Samuel Johnson was its landlord. By then it was an Ansell's tied house.

The Rose & Crown, at 28-9 Trent Street, closed on 30 December 1930. It was at the junction of Bordesley Street and dated from 1849. In Upper Trinity Street, which runs parallel to Bordesley High Street, was a beerhouse, the Castle Tavern, at No. 94.

It came up for auction on 30 May 1878, when it was revealed that it also possessed a brew-house and a stable. The Castle closed in 1914. The Greyhound was at No. 65, and dated from 1834, with Thomas Knowles as its first landlord. In 1890 the house was acquired by Ansells, and updated, rather than rebuilt, by James & Lister Lea. The Greyhound closed in 1919. Very much still there is the Clement Arms, in Upper Trinity Street. It was Grade II statutorily listed in December 1991, because of the many original features that it still contains, including its half-portioned bar and stained-glass windows.

At Watery Lane, before its redevelopment as Watery Lane Middleway, was the Sailor's Return at No. 3. It was reputedly paid for by the Vicar of Aston, Dr Spencer, and given to John Parkes, an ex-sailor who had served under his officer son at the Battle of the Nile. There was the Coachsmith's Arms at No. 27, a beerhouse which gained a full license in 1938; the Anchor, a licensed victuallers of 1862; the Barrel, at 182 Watery Lane, opened in 1862; and the Crown & Anchor at 222, opened in 1854. An Ansells house, it and the other pubs all closed for the construction of the Middleway.

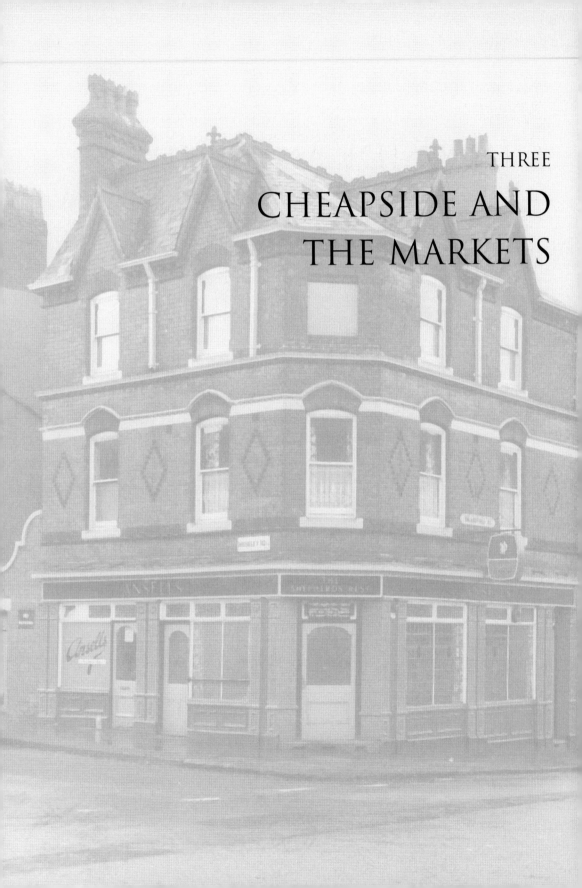

CHEAPSIDE AND THE MARKETS

THREE

CHEAPSIDE AND THE MARKETS

Cheapside leads off from the Markets, stretching from the south side of the parish church up to Camp Hill. It has two arterial roads, Bradford Street and Cheapside, and was developed from the late eighteenth century.

Bradford Street

On the corner of Moat Row and Bradford Street was the Birmingham Arms, originating in 1827. It was a markets pub, and had a 5.30 a.m. early morning license. Bought up by brewer William Butler, the old house was demolished and a new house was built, to the designs of well-known pub architects James & Lister Lea in August 1886. In the yard behind, accommodation for sixty horses was provided. At one time the pub was home to the Ancient Order of Druids and the Shakespeare Reading Society. The pub closed in 1973, and was demolished for the building of the present Wholesale Markets. Its replacement was the Mercat Cross for Scottish & Newcastle Breweries, opened on 21 May 1976. As ugly and brutal buildings go, it has few equals. Taken over by Ansells, its name was shortened to the Mercat. It is still ugly. Across the road on the other corner was the Drovers' Arms at 9 Moat Row/346 Bradford Street. It was an extended three-storey house of red brick and Welsh slate roof. Its name, which originated around 1850, is taken from the cattle drovers that took their beasts to the nearby market. The Drovers was taken over by M&B, and architect Henry Naden oversaw alterations in January 1890. Like the Birmingham Arms, it was demolished for the construction of the new market.

A few doors along from the Drovers was the Warwick Arms, at No. 323. James Gregg was licensee from 1828 to 1839. Brewers William Butler bought the house in 1870 and updated it. John Cooper Ward was the last landlord of this house, which closed in 1917.

The Birmingham Arms, Moat Row, 1971.

The Mercat Cross, a former Scottish & Newcastle house.

Above: *The Drovers' Arms, 1902. In the foreground is the old Rag Market.*

Opposite above: *The Anchor, Bradford Street.*

Opposite below: *The White Swan, Bradford Street.*

At 308 Bradford Street, on the corner of Rea Street, is the Grade II-listed Anchor, of 1902, designed by James & Lister Lea. The interior of this three-ale bar is a visual delight in Minton tiles and stained-glass windows. Now a free house, in 1996-7 and again in 1998-9 the Anchor was voted CAMRA Regional Pub of the Year. The present house replaced an earlier house, dating back to around 1785, under landlord John Bancroft, a builder. Across the road from the Anchor was the Greyhound, alias the Postage Stamp. A little further along the road is the White Swan, a Banks' house, at 276 Bradford Street. It was built at a cost of £2,000 to a design by James & Lister Lea, for brewers Ansells, in 1899. It is a typical Lea house in red brick and terracotta, and like the nearby Anchor, is decorated in Minton tiles, of cream, green, orange, crimson and turquoise. The main bar has leaded glass windows, and the bar itself is richly carved with a decorative back which includes two inlaid clocks.

The bar of the White Swan.

The Minton-tiled passageway of the White Swan.

The White Lion, at 96 Bradford Street, was built post-1750. It closed in 1863. The Golden Cup, also known as the Cup, opened in 1812 under William Tibbetts. He died in May 1816. The house was taken over by brewers Mills & Kendrick in 1854, and Ansells in 1896. The house closed in 1931. Its last licensee was Charles Brown. The Boars Head, not far from Camp Hill, originated in 1791. Situated originally at 183 Bradford Street the number later changed to 209. Thomas Cox, who died in February 1794, was its first licensee. This pub closed in 1920. Not so far away was the Royal William, at 274 Bradford Street. It was named after William IV, and opened in 1854. It appears to have changed its name to King William IV, and appears sporadically in the trade directories as such from 1869. It closed in 1914, upon the recommendation of the Licensing Justices. The licensee at the time received a miserly £5 in compensation for his troubles. There were three beerhouses, the Woodman, which surrendered its licence to the Justices in May 1909, the Royal George, modernised in April 1889, from the drawings of Franklin Cross, and surrendering its license in 1927, and the Hope & Anchor of 1860, under licensee Benjamin Palmer.

The Shepherds Rest, Bradford Street, 1966.

At the top end of Bradford Street, not far from St Anne's church, was the Shepherd's Rest, on the corner of Moseley Road. It was so-called because until the 1930s sheep and cattle arriving at Bordesley Station were driven down Bradford Street or Cheapside to the Meat Market. An old beerhouse taken over by Ansell's, Frederick Ballard purchased a full license for the pub in 1953, at a cost of £1,250. The Shepherd's Rest was pulled down in the 1980s, perhaps unnecessarily so, for its site remained vacant for over a decade. Across, on the other corner of Bradford Street and Warner Street, is the Adam & Eve. It was an old Ind Coope house. It dates from the 1820s under landlord Josiah Heath. Considerable alterations resulting in an almost total rebuild were carried out in 1889, under landlord William Young, from the plans of architect Franklin Cross. The Adam & Eve became an M&B house, but is now a free house, noted for its occasional live music.

Running parallel to the High Street and Bradford Street are Green Street and its continuation, Warwick Street. At 72 Green Street was the Hope & Anchor. The first recorded licensee, in 1821, was James Sheriden. About 1900 the house was taken over by Ansell's, who updated and refurbished it as a mock timber-framed house. The house was closed in 1933 as part of a general clear-out by the Justices of smaller back-street pubs. In Warwick Street, on the corner of Alcester Street is the Spotted Dog, now very much a traditional Irish house. It opened in 1865 under Henry Crutchley, was taken over by Ansell's and more or less completely rebuilt. In 1953, its landlord paid £1,450 for a full license. The Spotted Dog is now a free house. Now gone is the Handel's Head, first entered in the trade directory of 1818. The house is named after Anglo-German composer George Frederic Handel (1685–1759). The pub, by then over one hundred years old, closed in 1919. Lastly there was the White Swan at 90 Warwick Street. It was a beerhouse, listed in Kelly's Directories from 1937. The pub closed in 1958.

The Adam & Eve, Bradford Street, 1958.

The Spotted Dog, Warwick Street.

Cheapside

At the lower end of Cheapside, on the corner of Rea Street, was the Royal Oak. It was a Victorian beerhouse owned by Ansell's, and is first recorded, when it became a full public house, in the directory of 1938. George Willey was landlord then, up to 1957. The house closed in 1977. Further up the hill on the corner of Lombard Street is Cleary's, a free house. A former two-storey Ansell's house with a tall chimney, it began life as the Rose & Crown and dated back to 1810. The first known licensee was John Jeffries, whose death notice appears in the *Gazette* for Christmas Day 1815. Later in the century the pub became a Rushton's Brewery tied house. Rushton's brought in architect Francis Bristow on 7 September 1899 to draw up plans for the addition of a smoke room. In 1924 Rushton's were taken over by Ansell's. In the modern era the house was briefly known as Pall Mall, but following the collapse of Ansells was sold off and is now a free house. Across the road on the corner with Alcester Street is the Fountain. It was an Atkinson's house, taken over by M&B in 1959. It began life way back in 1780. Two years later the Deritend Building Society was established here on 7 January. The house was also used as the meeting place of the Trustees of Deritend Chapel. For more than half a century, between 1823 and 1879 the house was run by the Smith family; George, his wife Rebecca, their daughters Rebecca and Ann, and finally son George Henry Smith took charge.

Other houses along the street, now gone, include the Brushmakers Arms at No. 5, a former Butler's house, later acquired by Frederick Smith Ltd, who in turn were taken over by M&B. It gained a full license in 1951, at a cost of £800. The Brushmakers was demolished in 1972 for the building of the Wholesale Market. The Bricklayers Arms was at 40 Cheapside from around 1853 until 1898. Updates to the house were carried out from the 6 December 1882 plans of architect James Ravley jr. The Red Lion was at No. 64. It was opened post-1818 under licensee Joseph Smallwood. Architect Edward Holmes carried out work to the house in September 1890 for landlord Thomas Nicholls. The Red Lion closed in 1901. The curiously named Old English Gentleman was briefly at 228 Cheapside in the mid-1850s.

The Oxford Arms, a beerhouse, was updated to the designs of Frederick Charley, which were submitted for approval on 21 January 1885. Finally there was, at an unknown address in Cheapside, the Prince of Wales, which surrendered its license to the Justices in January 1907, as did the Swan with Two Necks. Apparently the premises were then used as an early morning adult school.

Leading off from Cheapside was Rea Street, with a pub called the Why Not, on the corner of Moseley Street. It was closed down by the Justices in 1912, its licensee, Bert Pickering, moved to the Waggon & Horses in Adderley Street. At 107 Rea Street was an unknown beerhouse run by Mrs Mary Vitey. In September 1882, Charles Wright drew-up plans for a new ground-floor front. Climbing the hill to Birchall Street, the next junction along Cheapside, there were three pubs here, all now gone. The Britannia was at 4 Birchall Street. Joseph Wilson was licensee from 1787 until his death in November 1804. The house closed under landlord Walter Stokes in 1901. The Dog & Duck, a beerhouse, was at No. 42, under Ann Jones in 1865. Then there was the Duke of Edinburgh, originating in 1875, under Charles Teale, which was closed by the Justices at the outbreak of the First World War.

In Lombard Street were two pubs, the Turk's Head at No. 17, and the Justice Tavern at 70 Lombard Street. The Turk's Head originated in 1828 under William Burgess, and closed in 1931, Fred Morris being its last landlord. The Justice Tavern opened in 1820 with Mordecai Giles as licensee, and closed in 1896. Alcester Street is now devoid of pubs, the last, the Dog,

Cleary's, formerly the Rose & Crown, Cheapside.

closed in 1976. It was a Victorian beerhouse, bought up by Rushton's pre-1903, and later taken over by Ansell's in 1924. The entrance to the cellar was through a trapdoor in front of the bar counter. When the draymen arrived there was a feeling of dread, in that there was a big hole in the floor, with large barrels rolling across the room ready to knock down any unsuspecting patron like a bowling pin, into the pit below. The Dog closed and became the Lighthouse Rescue Mission. The Compasses at 142 Alcester Street, down on the corner with Deritend High Street, was the birthplace of the nineteenth-century Glee Union, a musical society of some note. It opened in 1828 under Joseph Skinner. Briefly in the early 1860s the house was known as the Compass Vaults. Over 110 years old, this pub closed in 1937. The Dog & Partridge was at 17 Alcester Street. It was an 1840s house established by John Hill. Under John Holloway the house was updated by architect Charles J. Hodson in July 1880. The house fell victim to road widening in 1921. George Fenton was its last licensee. The Lamp was at an unknown address in Alcester Street in 1767, under landlady the Widow Cope. Of the last public house, the Phoenix, there from post-1823 to 1836, three licensees are listed, John Holmes, Francis Roberts and Hannah Richardson.

Moseley Street

Running parallel to Cheapside is Moseley Street. There is one classic pub here, the Market Tavern, situated on the corner of Birchall Street. It began life as the Minerva, back in the late eighteenth century. By 1827 it had changed its name to the Dog & Partridge. It was taken over by the Holt Brewery of Aston, and demolished. A new public house, designed by James & Lister Lea, was built in the following year at a cost of £1,000. It is a typical Lea pub, built in red brick and terracotta, with an oriel window, topped by a small turret, above its corner entrance. In 1934 the Dog & Partridge was acquired by Ansell's when they took over Holt's. In 1984 there was a fire which completely gutted the top two floors. The house was carefully restored, and in the process the hardboard and studding added in the 1960s was removed to reveal the original buff and blue tiles beneath. The house re-opened on 3 April 1986, under new owners Pubmaster. It is rightly Grade II listed.

At 128 Moseley Street is the Hen & Chickens, dating from around 1855. It was bought up by the Holt Brewery, who employed Joseph Hidkin in June 1878 to update it. Curiously, when the brewery were taken over by Ansell's, the Hen & Chickens became an M&B pub. It was at one time renamed the Brewers Arms, but has now reverted to its original name. At 1 Moseley Street, on the corner of Sherlock Street, was the New Inn, opened in 1853 under licensee John King. In 1858 the house was renamed the Eagle & Ball, George Docker was in charge. It closed in 1971. The Birmingham Horse, at No. 21, was a former beerhouse, taking its name from a race horse called Birmingham. In 1830 it was entered as a three-year-old

The Market Tavern, Moseley Street.

Window detail, Market Tavern.

in the St Leger, by its owner, John Beardsworth, who ran a horse repository in Moseley Street. Ridden by a jockey by the name of Connolly, the horse won, with prize money of £1,760, plus side bets. As a reward, Beardsworth gave the jockey £500. The Birmingham Horse was taken over by Atkinson's who brought in architect Hiram Wilcox in 1891 to update the house, He produced a neat, yet unassuming two-storey house, faced in stone on its ground-floor level. The house was later acquired by M&B, and in 1951, licensee Walter Watts purchased a full license for the Birmingham Horse at a cost of £1,000. This pub closed on 20 December 1970 for the construction of the new Wholesale Market.

The Apollo Tavern was a two-storey castellated Georgian house with scallop surrounds to the upper windows, and a central door with columns. Situated on the bank of the river Rea, it came into being around 1785. It was advertised as a pleasure resort, being barely half an hour's walk from the centre of the town. It had little success as a public house, and was converted into a private house by its new owner, the Birmingham historian William Hamper, in the mid-nineteenth century. The Daniel Lambert was situated on the corner of Moseley Street and Lombard Street. This beerhouse had a pub sign depicting the very obese young Leicestershire man, Daniel Lambert, who gained fame because he was obese. By the age of twenty-three he was thirty-two stone. At one time he was apprenticed to the Birmingham firm of John Taylor & Co. of Church Street. Lambert died in 1810, at the age of forty. Six doors up from the Daniel Lambert, at 65 Moseley Street, was the Talbot, a beerhouse, shown on the Rating Maps of 1870. The Audrey Arms, an M&B tied house, which closed in 1980, was situated at 88 Moseley Street, on the corner of Alcester Street.

Above: *The Fountain, Cheapside, 1984.*

Opposite: *The Hen & Chickens, Moseley Street.*

It was a former beerhouse, only gaining a full license in 1921. At 119 Moseley Street was the Quiet Woman, whose inn sign depicted a woman with her decapitated head under her arm. A beerhouse, it was in existence in 1862, reputedly re-named the Good Woman. The Swan at 141 Moseley Street dated from 1820, and closed in 1852. The White Swan, at 184 Moseley Street, dated from 1840. John Rudge was the first listed licensee. The house closed in 1921, under its last licensee, Arthur Lewis.

The Old Plough, a beerhouse at 232 Moseley Street, was leased by owners, the Granger Estate, to Rushton's Lion Brewery of Aston, in 1905, at an annual rent of £38 per annum. Rushton's were later taken over by Ansell's in 1924. The Castle, another beerhouse, was updated by architect, J.J. Raggett in June 1898. It was obliged to surrender its license to the Justices in May 1908. The White Horse, updated by Arthur Hamblin in July 1895, surrendered its license in 1912. The Plough & Harrow, on the corner of Moseley and Rea Streets, was ignominiously turned into a café.

Camp Hill

The Ship Inn, at Camp Hill, was a timber-framed one-and-a-half-storey house, later encased in brick. An oak beam over the fireplace bore the date of 1560. The house was originally known as the Anchor, and was allegedly the headquarters of Prince Rupert, prior to his assault upon Birmingham in 1643. The change in name took place in 1796, under licensee Frederick Wood. The house was closed in 1869, demolished, and replaced by a new three-storey Ship Hotel. Later acquired by Ansell's, it was closed in 1969 and remained boarded up until its demolition in the summer of 1971 for road re-alignment at Camp Hill. Further down the road near Holy Trinity church was the Bull's Head, a little M&B pub. It was the second house on the site, the first dated from 1728. The second house, a curious single-storey building, was added onto the front of an early nineteenth-century end-of-terrace house. The Bull's Head closed on 2 November 1975. At nearby Warner Street was the Harvest Home, now gone, a beerhouse updated from plans submitted by Henry T. Mills on 27 February 1878. At 55 Ravenhurst Street was the Salutation, opened in 1861. The last entry is in 1865. At 77 was the Bell, dating from 1839. This beerhouse closed on 29 June 1926. Still very much here is the Moseley Arms at 105 Ravenhurst Street. Samuel Fisher was its first landlord from 1835 to 1850. Robert Atherton drew-up plans for the house's modernisation in April 1885. It was taken over by M&B. but is now a free house. The Brewer & Baker is a Victorian house, once owned by M&B. It was noted for serving Highgate Mild during the winter, as well as Springfield Bitter all year around; an ideal lunchtime pint. The front of the building was rebuilt to its original state for safety reasons in the 1990s.

Above: *The Ship Inn, Camp Hill, 1869.*

Left: *The Bull's Head, Camp Hill, 1968.*

The Ship Hotel, Camp Hill, c. 1947.

Above: *The Moseley Arms, Ravenhurst Street.*

Left: *The Brewer & Baker, Camp Hill.*

The Markets Area

The old Markets area, now largely disappeared beneath the 1970s Wholesale Markets complex, was bounded by Edgbaston Street, Moat Lane, Moat Row, Bromsgrove Street and Pershore Street, and included within it Jamaica Row, Gloucester Street, Dean Street and Upper Dean Street.

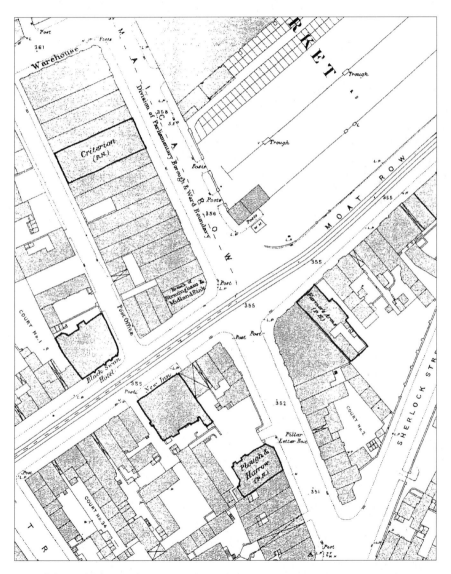

Map of the Markets area, 1887.

The Brewer & Baker was in Moat Lane. An early nineteenth-century house, alterations and additions were made here following S.W. Mountford's submission of plans on 27 February 1885. The license of the Brewer & Baker was surrendered to the Justices in 1928, and market warehouses were built on the site.

One door up from Jamaica Row was the Farmer's Arms, a narrow-fronted three-storey brick-built Georgian house. In 1886 it was rebuilt to the designs of James & Lister Lea. A beerhouse, it surrendered up its license in 1932. Just off Moat Row, in Smithfield Street, were two pubs, the Oxford & Cambridge and the Ram Inn. The Oxford & Cambridge opened in 1891. Alfred Greenfield was its first licensee. The house closed in 1898. The Ram was an old Markets pub, dating from 1838, with an early morning license.

The Black Boy Stores in Jamaica Row was an extension of the Black Boy in St Martin's Lane. It was built by John Gough for the tanners and cattle drovers, that they might be accommodated with food and drink without interfering with his more respectable trade. The license was given up under the Improvement Scheme on the Gooch Estate. Also losing their license in 1892 were the Fisherman's Arms, the Red Cow and the Woodman's Stores, situated at the end of a terrace of early eighteenth-century houses. At 13 Jamaica Row was the Smithfield Arms, originating around 1860. A second house, in the Queen Anne style, was built on the site, to the designs of James & Lister Lea in 1885. In 1950, licensee Doris Caldicott obtained a full license at a cost of £1,475. This pub was demolished for the 1970s Market.

The Criterion Vaults, originally Brookes Wine & Spirit Vaults, dating from 1865, was bought by William Jones in 1883, to add to his Criterion pub company. The house had a back entrance onto Market Street, with an early morning license for the sale of rum and coffee to market workers. In 1885 the house was sold to emerging Aston brewers, Atkinsons. They brought in James & Lister Lea to completely redesign the house in the Flemish style. Renamed Brook Vaults, it opened in January 1886. Inside the seating was unusual in that it had long leather-covered benches, which were divided by arms into individual seats. Quite unique in Birmingham. The house was compulsorily purchased by the City Council in 1970 and demolished in 1974 for the construction of the Wholesale Markets. The Plough & Harrow was at 81 Jamaica Row. In 1887, favourite pub architects James & Lister Lea designed a new house in the Old English style; a half-timbered construction. The Cross Keys, down on the corner of Sherlock Street, opened in 1885. Like the Plough & Harrow, and so many other pubs in this area, it was closed in 1970 for the new Market. At Balsall Street, the road that linked Jamaica Row and Cheapside, was the Cross Keys, at No. 9. It originated in the early 1820s, Joseph Field is its first known licensee in 1823. The house was pulled down for the earlier Wholesale Market of 1881.

In Gloucester Street was the Old Rose & Crown where reputedly, in the mid-eighteenth century, the Revd Dr Crofts of St Martin's held his churchwardens' meetings. The Welcome Inn was a beerhouse in Dean Street. It was rebuilt in 1891 from plans drawn-up by master pub architects James & Lister Lea. The license of the inn was withdrawn in 1929. The Coach & Horses at 40 Upper Dean Street opened in 1840. It was bought by Fulford's Brewery of Holt Street, Gosta Green, later to become the Holt Brewery in 1886 when Henry Fulford's brother-in-law, W.L. Hodgkinson, reconstituted the business. The house was compulsorily purchased in 1926 and demolished to provide extra warehouse space for the markets.

Brooks Vaults, Jamaica Row, 1924.

BLACK SWAN INN,

BROMSGROVE STREET, BIRMINGHAM,

CHARLES HODGES . . . Proprietor.

Choice Wines and Spirits direct from the Docks,

FINE HOME-BREWED BURTON AND BITTER ALES,

DRAUGHT & BOTTLED PORTER, &c.

An Ordinary every Tuesday and Thursday at One o'clock.

A £5 CLUB HELD EVERY MONDAY EVENING. BEDS.

Above: *The Dolphin Inn, later the Australian Bar, from an advertisement of 1850.*

Opposite above: *A Victorian advertisement for the Black Swan.*

Opposite below: *The Stag & Pheasant, Bromsgrove Street, 1924.*

Above: *The remains of the Rose & Crown, Lower Essex Street.*

Opposite: *The King's Arms, Pershore Street, 1924.*

Bromsgrove Street runs from Moat Row in the Markets district, all the way down to Bristol Street. For convenience its full length is covered here. At 8 Bromsgrove Street was the Black Swan, on the corner of Market Street. It was an early eighteenth-century house, rebuilt in 1886 from the plans submitted by James & Lister Lea on 11 December 1885. The house was noted as being the headquarters of the Butchers' Sick & Dividend Society, established by landlord William Ball, himself a former butcher. It too closed in 1970 for the new Market. Across the road from this pub was the New Inn, at 191-194 Bromsgrove Street. Originally built in the Georgian era, it too was replaced by a James & Lister Lea house, in the Old English style, from their plans of 28 August 1884. In 1934 the New Inn was taken over by M&B. It closed in 1972. The Stag & Pheasant was at 32 Bromsgrove Street, on the corner with Pershore Street. Samuel Davis was its first known licensee, in 1835. Later in the century it became a Holt's pub, and in 1924 was taken over by Ansell's. It closed four years later, in 1928. On the next corner of Bromsgrove Street and Hurst Street was the Dolphin, a three-storey Georgian house, with a stable at the rear. During the 1840s and '50s it was also used as an auction house by owner Samuel Rodway. Later in the nineteenth century the house changed its name to the Australian Gin Palace under Thomas Hicks, and evolved into the Australian Bar.

The Hop Pole, Pershore Street, 1924.

A bit of a curiosity was the Globe Tavern in Bromsgrove Street. It was noted in 1855, under John Faulkner, for having a pear tree in front. In 1926, three beerhouses in Bromsgrove Street were closed; the Royal George, the Ring of Bells and the Maid & Magpie, that had been updated by lesser-known pub architect, George Ravenscroft, in July 1882. A second minor pub architect, J. Dainty, drew-up plans for the updating of a beerhouse called the Reaper, on 19 March 1888. Only second to James & Lister Lea was William Jenkins, who updated the Malt Shovel from his plans of 31 December 1883. The Black Horse, another beerhouse, is recorded with its closure under an Improvement Scheme on the Gooch estate in 1892. At the far end of Bromsgrove Street, on the corner of Essex Street, is the boarded-up Rose & Crown, at 135 Bromsgrove Street. A magnificent four-storey red-brick house, it was designed by William Jenkins in 1901 for William Butler's Brewery. It closed in 1956, was taken up by the TUC, and became a trade union headquarters, renamed Unity House. Later closed, plans were put forward in November 1991 to re-establish the premises as a pub. Apart from the bar, all fixtures and fittings were still intact. However these plans came to nothing. This Jenkins-designed house replaced an earlier pub on the site, dating from 1791, under licensee John Pitchfork. By way of replacement for these pubs is the Missing Bar, a modern pub on the edge of the Gay Quarter.

Pershore Street leads off from Edgbaston Street, eventually linking up with Bromsgrove

Street. At 13-15 Pershore Street was the Britannia Stores. A beerhouse, it opened in 1880 and closed in 1936. There were two 1860s beerhouses, both of which are now gone, the Nelson of 1865 and the Travellers Rest of 1864. The King's Arms was at 22 Pershore Street, opposite Smithfield Passage. It dated from 1849, under James Birch. William Jenkins updated it from his plans of 8 September 1887 for the Holt Brewery. The house was closed in 1929, the land acquired for Markets warehousing. Up on the corner of Upper Dean Street was the Hop Pole at 41-43 Pershore Street. Dating from around 1840 under John Brown, it was updated by William Jenkins for owners Holt's Brewery from his plans of 10 June 1884. In 1928 the house gained a full license. The Hop Pole was torn down in 1972 for the construction of the present Markets. There has been one post-Markets pub, the Wonder Bar, which boasts a late night license.

Sherlock Street runs from Moat Row all the way down to Belgrave Road. At 24-5 Sherlock Street was the White Hart, originating around 1842. Charles J. Hodson carried out alterations to the house from his plans of 17 July 1878. The White Hart closed in 1937. At 62 was the Crown & Anchor, dating from 1855. It apparently closed in 1869. The Woodman was at 86, a house dating from 1850. It closed 110 years later, in 1960, and its license was transferred to a pub in Shard End. At 124 Sherlock Street was the Coach & Horses, a post-1872 pub, which closed in 1896. The Odd Fellows Arms is a narrow-fronted Ansell's house of three storeys, at 135 Sherlock Street. It gained a full license in 1937. The King's Arms at 171 was situated on the corner of Benacre Street. Its first licensee was John Cartwright in 1865. The house was closed in the late 1960s for road widening. At 230 Sherlock Street was the Swan, a house dating from the late 1840s. It closed in 1938. The White Swan, a noted home-brew house, opened in 1840. G.R. Faulkner carried out

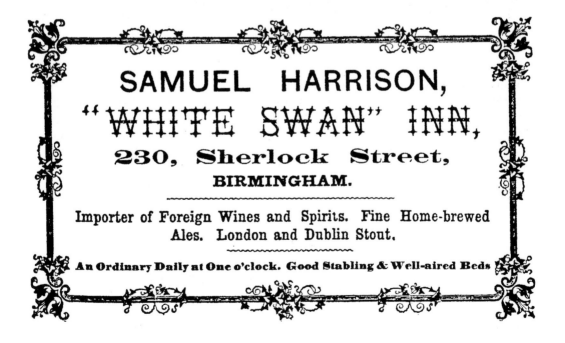

A Victorian advertisement for the White Swan, Pershore Street.

Above: *The Queen's Arms, Barford Street.*

Left: *The Lamp, Barford Street.*

alterations from 15 July 1895. In 1937 architect J.B. Surman carried out further updating. This pub, at the junction of Pershore Road, was demolished in the 1970s. There were a number of beerhouses along Sherlock Street. The Cheltenham Arms surrendered its license in 1907, and the Burton Stores in 1909. Both the Stanley Arms and the Ryland Arms closed in 1927, and the Five Ways Inn closed in 1930.

Just off Sherlock Street is Bishop Street. The Queen's Head at No. 20 originated in 1851, and closed seventy years later in 1921. The Rose, a beerhouse, closed in May 1908. The Swan, another beerhouse, closed in June 1910. The White Horse was updated by prominent Birmingham architect W.H. Ward in October 1888, but it too has now gone. The Red Lion, a beerhouse dating from the eighteenth century, was closed in 1912. The Mitre, on the corner of Lower Hurst Street, was updated by William Jenkins in August 1887. It closed on 31 December 1927. In Barford Street there was a plethora of pubs, most of them gone by the slum clearance of the area in the late 1960s. The King's Arms of 1823 closed on 17 March 1928. It was an old Davenport's house, taken over by them in 1903. The Vulcan at 37 was equally as old, obtaining a full license in 1841. It closed in 1900. Right next door was the Roebuck at 39, shown on the Rating Maps of 1870. The Lamb was at 157 Barford Street. It closed in 1971. The Queen Arms at 160 Barford Street, on the corner of Macdonald Street, first opened in 1852, and is still going strong as a free house. There were two beerhouses, the Nelson, which closed in May 1922 and the Stag & Pheasant, which closed on 17 March 1928. The Lamp is still there. At one time it was Birmingham's smallest pub. It was voted the city branch of CAMRA's Pub of the Year in 1994 and 1997. It is the only regular outlet in the city for the Cotswold brewer Stanway's Stanney Bitter.

The next road along is Bissell Street. There were two beerhouses here, the Royal Exchange which closed in June 1910, and the General Wyndham which closed in 1926. Very briefly in Wrentham Street was the Earl Grey of 1840-42, under landlord Charles Cluleee. A second Earl Grey was later opened along the Pershore Road. Just below Wrentham Street was Benacre Street, now completely cleared. At 127 Benacre Street was the Roebuck, an old Kelsey's house, later taken over by Ansell's. It dated from 1850, and closed in 1941. Both the Globe and the Packhorse, two old beerhouses, were closed by the Licensing Justices in 1912 as part of the 'fewer but better' scheme. The Anchor, a third beerhouse, closed in 1957.

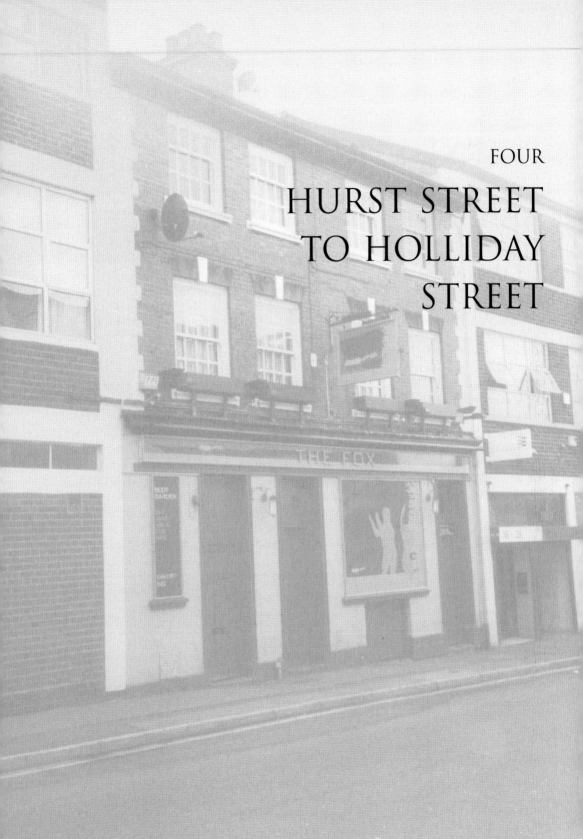

FOUR

HURST STREET TO
HOLLIDAY STREET

Hurst Street and Surrounds

Hurst Street is now part of the Gay Quarter of the city. Near to its corner with Thorp Street was the post-Inner Ring Road Windmill, opened in July 1966. An M&B pub, it was approached down a flight of stairs. A little more interesting perhaps is the Old Fox, on the corner of 55 Inge Street. It was established around 1813, John Weale being its first landlord. During the early 1860s it was known as the Fox Inn & Freemasons' Tavern, but by 1865 had reverted to its original name. The Old Fox was taken over by the Holt Brewery in 1892. The original house was demolished, and James & Lister Lea drew-up plans on 21 March 1892 for its replacement. This is the house we see today. It is quite unlike the majority of Lea-designed pubs. Just across the road from the Birmingham Hippodrome, it is claimed that Charlie Chaplin, while touring with Fred Karno's Army, drank here. During the 1970s the pub was extended at the rear to provide an extra large room.. In the following decade the Old Fox was threatened with demolition. In 1987 the Gooch Estate, who own the land, put forward a plan for a £30 million redevelopment of the area. Following considerable pressure, including a 600-name petition, the City Council gave outline planning permission for development, on the basis that the Old Fox should remain.

On the other corner of Hurst Street and Thorp Street was the Lord Rodney. The house, originally known as the Rodney Tavern, dates from around 1820. In 1879 it was taken over by William Jones and added to his Criterion Pub chain. The house was apparently largely rebuilt under Jones. With the collapse of his empire, the house was taken over by Atkinson's Brewery and its name changed back. It was obliged to surrender its license to the Justices in 1939. Richard Wood, there from 1934, was its last landlord.

Right down the bottom of Thorp Street, on the corner of the Horse Fair, is the White Lion, a former Davenport's pub. The pub was designed by James & Lister Lea in 1896, creating an imposing French Empire-style house with wrought-iron balconies on its upper storey, the whole surmounted by a small clock tower. This house replaced an earlier pub on the site dating from 1821, with Charles Kempster as its first licensee. The Australian, as it is known today, is on the corner of Bromsgrove Street. The house was originally known

Mr. & Mrs. D. G. Hadland
welcome you to the

Windmill

Albany House, Hurst Street

This new Bass, M&B house,
adjacent to the Hippodrome,
(Birmingham Theatre) offers
a fine selection of high quality snacks, lunch times and
evenings, before and after
the theatre, as well as your
favourite brew from

BASS ▲ M & B
WORTHINGTON

Bass, Mitchells & Butlers Limited

Right: *Opening advertisement for the Windmill, Hurst Street.*

Below: *The Old Fox, Hurst Street.*

The Lord Rodney, Hurst Street, 1924.

as the Dolphin, dating back to the late eighteenth century. Under landlord Thomas Hicks, in 1855, the house was renamed the Australian Gin Palace, a name commemorating the Australian Gold Rush. In 1897 the pub was taken over by Davenport's. They brought in James & Lister Lea, who drew-up plans on 6 April 1897 for its re-build. The name evolved into the Australian Palace, and in 1939 it became the Australian Bar. Following Davenport's takeover by Greenall Whitley, the Aussie Bar's two rooms were knocked into one. It is now a free house. The Roebuck, further down Hurst Street, on the corner of Skinner Lane, is now known as the Village Inn. An early nineteenth-century converted domestic house, further alterations were carried out based on C.J. Hodson's plans of 19 October 1887. The house was later acquired by M&B, but was sold off, and is now a free house. It has a regular entry in the CAMRA Good Beer Guide. Down Skinner Lane was the Nelson at No. 46. Robert Bruce was landlord when it opened in 1853. Alterations and additions were carried out by Charles J. Hodson (25 October 1878) and Jones & Mason in 1890. The Nelson closed in 1929 for new warehousing.

Now gone is the Cross Keys, at 18 Hurst Street. Designed for Ansell's by architect H.W. Hobbiss, it resembled more an art deco cinema than a pub. The building was faced in golden Siena marble, and above the first floor was a wedge-shaped column topped by a decorative pylon. The work was carried out by the Birmingham Guild. The Cross Keys was demolished

The Australian Bar, Hurst Street, 1985.

Above: *The Roebuck, Hurst Street, 1984.*

Opposite above: *52 Degrees North (the geographical location of Birmingham), Hurst Street.*

Opposite below: *PJ's Moon & Sixpence, Arcadian Centre.*

in the 1960s, a victim of Herbert Manzoni's Inner Ring Road. At 29 Hurst Street was the Hope & Anchor, established by 1814 under landlord William Garnett. The house closed in 1857. At 31-2 Hurst Street was the Anchor, dating from around 1839. It was taken over by William Freeman in 1859 and renamed the Black Lion. It closed in 1939. The Gooch Arms was at 36, and opened by 1853. Its licence was withdrawn in 1929. Three beerhouses: the Forresters opened in 1908 and closed in 1928, the Unicorn, revamped from Charles Hodson's plans of 3 November 1879, and now closed, as is the Rose & Crown, rebuilt from William Jenkin's plans of 1900, as a four-storey house with barge-board gables. Their replacements include Route Two, with a six-day late night license, and 52 Degrees North (the geographical location of Birmingham). It is an eye-catching modern building, being part of the Arcadian development. It was opened in 1998 by Piers Sanderson. Adjoining is PJ's Moon & Sixpence, opened in March 1992. A free house, the pipes to the beer-pumps form part of the décor. Pat O'Connells in the Arcadian Centre was an Irish theme pub from the 1990s, later taken over by the O'Neill chain – equally cod-Irish.

The Compasses in Inge Street was a Pindar & Co. Junction Brewery public house. Built in a converted late eighteenth-century house, in the 1860s and '70s it had a reputation for staging dog fights and ratting matches. The Compasses was demolished in 1894 as part of

The Compasses, Inge Street.

an Improvement Scheme for the area. At 11 Inge Street was the Barrel Inn, again dating from the late eighteenth century. It was a beerhouse; James Shelton was landlord in 1796. It closed in 1895. The Robin Hood, also now gone, was at 11 Inge Street about the same time. The replacement for these lost pubs is the Crow's Nest Theatre Bar, on the corner of Inge Street and Essex Street. It has a nautical theme in its décor, but is saved by the fact that it sells Lowenbrau. On the opposing corner with Essex Street is the Queen's Tavern. It is a subdued James & Lister Lea house, designed for Ansell's on 8 November 1894. Now a free house, inside it consists of high-ceilinged rooms, with large cut-glass windows. At 7 Essex Street was the Royal Oak, situated between Inge and Bromsgrove Streets. There was a beerhouse here, the Apple Tree. It surrendered its license to the Justices in May 1908. In Lower Essex Street was the Lamp, at No. 8, which closed in 1940. The White Horse, an Ansell's pub, was at 17 Lower Essex Street. It is described in Kelly's Directory of 1940 as 'a public house without a sign'. The Fox, in Lower Essex Street, is a former Ansell's house, with a beer garden in the rear. Of late the exterior has been painted in a somewhat striking manner. On the edge of the Gay Quarter, it attracts a lesbian clientele. Lastly there was the Fountain, a beerhouse that surrendered its license to the Justices in May 1908. Its landlord received £100 in compensation. Crossing Lower Essex Street is Kent Street. There were two pubs here, both casualties of the slum clearances. The Princess Alexandra was at 27 Kent Street and closed in 1972. The Fountain, an old three-roomed house, was an Ansell's pub.

The Crow's Nest, Inge Street.

Gooch Street and Gooch Street North stretch from Bromsgrove Street all the way down to Belgrave Middleway. At 41 was the Queen's Head, opened in 1864, and closed by the Justices in 1927. The Rodney was at 60 Gooch Street. An old beerhouse, it closed in 1940, unable to get the necessary supplies for beer production. The White Star was at 109. It dated from the 1850s under William Charley. It closed as part of a general clearance of slum housing in 1967. The Garrick's Head of 1858, at 180 Gooch Street, was renamed the Duke of Wellington in 1868. It was closed by the Justices as part of the 'fewer but better scheme' in 1936. At 242 Gooch Street was the Red Cow, a beerhouse situated on the corner of Kent Street. There by 1870, it surrendered its license in 1912. Situated on the other corner was the Bath Tavern of 1854, closing in 1974. The Bridge Tavern was at 273. A beerhouse, it gained a full license in 1916. It was closed down in 1941. Way down on the corner of Belgrave Road was the Clement Arms. Established by 1897, it was demolished for the cutting of Belgrave Middleway. Of the survivors there is the British Oak, at 77 Gooch Street North. A beerhouse, it gained a full license in 1938. The Wellington is on the corner of Bishop Street. An old M&B house it is situated between a sixties housing estate and an industrial estate, and draws custom from both. Lastly there is the Sir Charles Napier at 155 Gooch Street. It opened in 1857, with John Brown as landlord. It survived the slum clearance of the late 1960s, and since then a new estate has grown up around it.

Above: *Window detail, the Queen's Tavern.*

Left: *The Fox, Essex Street.*

Above: *The British Oak, Gooch Street North.*

Right: *The Queen's Tavern, Inge Street and Essex Street corner.*

The Horse Fair and Bristol Street

Brick Kiln Lane was the original name of the Horse Fair. At No. 1 was the Plow & Harrow, a house dating from 1767. Henry Clare was landlord. He was followed by John Deakin in 1777. Not too far away was another pub dating from this period, the Lamp. Edward Cooper was its landlord during this time. The change in name to the Horse Fair took place in 1812. At 8 Horse Fair, as it now was, situated on the corner of Windmill Street, was the Duke of York. It dated from around 1803, John Powis is listed as licensee by 1818. Under landlord James Sandland, the house was rebuilt as a three-storey pub with an entrance on the corner. It possessed a bar, smoke room and out-door. On the first floor were two living rooms and a kitchen with tip-up bath. On the second floor were two bedrooms. Out in the yard behind was a urinal and wc. It was a very functional establishment, state of the art, catering for the expectations of the day. The Duke was de-licensed in March 1937. Edith Arnett was its last licensee. The premises were cleared in the 1960s during road widening. The Golden Lion was at 8 Horse Fair, though this is probably a case of street re-numbering.

Above: *The Brown Lion, Horse Fair, 1924.*

Opposite: *The Duke of York, corner of Horse Fair &and Windmill Street, 1924.*

BALSALL HEATH

BUILDING ESTATE.

TO

BE SOLD BY AUCTION,

BY E. & C. ROBINS,

ON FRIDAY, THE 27th DAY OF JUNE, 1834,

At the Bell Inn, Bristol-street,

AT THREE O'CLOCK IN THE AFTERNOON, A NUMBER OF LOTS OF

Building Land,

Forming part of the Estate of Messrs. EDWARDS,

SITUATE AT BALSALL HEATH,

In the Hamlet of Moseley, in the County of Worcester, close to Birmingham, including Frontages to

TINDAL-STREET AND GEORGE-STREET;

ALSO SOME LOTS ADJOINING THE RESIDENCES OF

J. T. LAWRENCE, Esq. Mr. T. GILBERT, AND Mrs. POTTS;

ALSO COMPRISING THE

FARM HOUSE,

With SEVERAL ACRES OF LAND surrounding it.

The whole of the intended Lots are elevated and the Scenery most beautiful.

The NEW LINES OF ROAD now formed ACROSS THIS ESTATE, have given facilities for BUILDING unequalled in this Neighbourhood, and have brought the Lots within a few minutes' walk of the CENTRE OF THE TOWN, which are distinguished by staves with painted numbers on them.

Other information may be had of Mr. MOLE, Solicitor, Carr's-lane, and of Messrs. E. and C. ROBINS, Auctioneers, New-street Birmingham.

J. TOMKINSON, PRINTER, 39, SNOW-HILL, BIRMINGHAM.

Above: *Sales particulars of an auction at the Bell, Bristol Street.*

Opposite above: *The Red Cow, Horse Fair, 1962.*

Opposite below: *Scot's Arms, Bristol Street, 1924.*

Familiar Figures.—137.

"Johnny" McInnes—he is invariably called "Johnny," and never John—is a very popular member of the licensed trade in Birmingham. He has had more than one haunt; his present one is at the corner of Bristol-street and Bromsgrove-street, and a very fine old country house it must have been when what is known as "The Bank," in the Horse Fair, was a series of prettily-terraced gardens. "Johnny" McInnes has always borne himself irreproachably, and numbers among his best friends many of Birmingham's prominent citizens. He has a good presence, and has in his time played many parts.

Johnny McInness, landlord of the Wellington, 1902.

Henry Harris was landlord in 1835. The Brown Lion was across the road at the junction of Essex Street. It dated from 1818. In 1879-80, the house was updated to the plans of Osborn & Reading. James Fox bought the house to add to his portfolio of pubs around the city. Upon his death in 1891, the pub was offered for sale and was purchased as an investment by Messrs Colerick, Bird & Co., and leased out. The Brown Lion closed in 1939. At 13 Horse Fair was the Dun Cow, depicted though not named on Thomas Hanson's Plan of Birmingham for 1778. It closed in 1866, near enough 100 years old. At 23-24 Horse Fair, right next door to the old Roman Catholic church of St Catherine's, was the Red Cow, a late eighteenth-century three-storey house dating from 1785 with Edward Cooper as landlord. It was updated by William Jenkins from his plans of 1 November 1877. William Butler's Brewery took over the pub, and it later became an M&B house. The pub was closed in 1963, along with the church next door and other buildings along this side of the road. They were demolished for road widening.

The Bell Inn, Bristol Street, 1965.

The Victoria Inn, Bristol Street, 1964.

Bristol Street is the continuation of the Horse Fair. At No. 19, on the corner of Irving Street, was the Scott's Arms. It was a beerhouse, shown on the Rating Maps of 1870. By the turn of the century it had become an M&B tied house. It was obliged to surrender its licenses to the Justices on 31 December 1927, as part of the city's 'fewer but better' policy. The Bell, along Bristol Street, was situated on the corner of Bell Barn Road. It was designed by James & Lister Lea in 1886 for Butler's Brewery. Their red brick and terracotta public house replaced an earlier one of the same name, dating back at least to 1795. Its address was then 23 Bristol Street. After the rebuild the address was changed to 57-59, and later 356 Bristol Street. The Bell was closed in the late 1960s for road widening along this stretch of Bristol Street. Across on the other side of the road is the Wellington, at 212 Bristol Street. It was built around 1815, its first licensee was Richard Parsons. Alterations and additions were carried out by James & Lister Lea, following plans submitted on 10 September 1890. Their design was a very convincing Regency style, added onto the original Georgian house. Further updating occurred in 1914, under popular landlord John McInnes. He placed an advertisement in the *Birmingham Echo*, during January 1915:

> JOHNNY McINNES, Wellington Hotel, Bristol St. (Corner of Bromsgrove Street),
> Telephone:- 927 Midland. Fully Licensed. Specialty – Bitter Drawn from the Wood.
> Thoroughly renovated throughout. Comfortable Smoke Room. Good Billiard Room.
> The House of Call.

The Wellington survived the changes of the 1960s and remains as a popular public house along this stretch of Bristol Street.

The Victoria, yet another James & Lister Lea designed house, was at 193 Bristol Street. It was designed for M&B in a quiet, restrained manner; neat, but outstanding. The house was three storeys in height with a large centrally placed window, with doors either side. Suspended from the first floor was a large lantern. The Victoria too fell victim to the Bristol Street widening scheme of 1964-65. The Sun, at 217-19 Bristol Street, faced onto St Luke's church. Henry Naden oversaw the rebuild of the house in May 1887, later adding a billiard room in the August of that year. His house replaced an earlier pub dating back to 1827. M&B took over the Sun in 1898, which, like many other Bristol Street pubs, closed in the 1960s. Also closed at this time was the Nottingham Arms at 147 Bristol Street, on the corner of Bristol Passage.

The New Inn was a late eighteenth-century beerhouse. A 'Mrs Ryland', its landlady, died here on 11 December 1791. The Stores had a beer and wine license. Following negotiations with the Licensing Justices, it closed on 13 October 1925. The licensee received £1,640 in compensation. The Stafford Arms, another beerhouse, was updated under the direction of Robert Matthews, who submitted plans on 26 December 1891. The Stafford Arms was obliged to surrender its license in 1928.

Leading off from Bristol Street is Great Colmore Street, redeveloped as part of the Lee Bank estate in the 1960s. All the public houses, if not gone by that date, were then swept away. The Royal Oak, a little-known beerhouse, closed in 1914. The Vine, at 77 Great Colmore Street, dated from 1848 under licensee Watson Langton. It was closed in 1878. The Hop Pole on the corner of Irving Street, dating from 1859, closed in 1931 as part of a periodic general closure of public houses by the Justices. The White Horse, at 250, also dated from the 1850s. It became a Holt's house, later taken over by Ansells in 1924. While under Holt's, William Jenkins was called in to update it from his plans of 8 July 1899.

The Edgbaston Tavern, Bristol Street, 1964.

The White Horse closed in May 1959. Its license was transferred to the Mackadown in Sheldon. The Grand Junction of 1867 was closed in 1960. The Shakespearian Bar, once part of the Fox & Co. pub company, closed in 1961. The replacement for these closures was the Colwyn, a basic Ansell's house.

Latimer Street, now gone beneath the Lee Bank development of the 1960s, had five beer/public houses; the White Hart, a beerhouse, with new stables added in August 1899 by architect William Hinson, the Red Lion, which closed on 31 December 1935 (the 'fewer but better' scheme), The Wheatsheaf at 138 closed in 1956, the Colmore Arms closed in 1961, and the Barley Mow, opened in 1870, updated by Joseph Fidkin (15 May 1879) and closed in 1922. Irving Street, which has largely survived the changes of the 1960s, lost most of its pub before that date. The Fountain closed in 1922, the Three Horse Shoes closed in 1936, and the Coach & Horses, opened in 1854, closed in 1938. Those that were closed for the new estate were the Nag's Head, modernised by William Jenkins from his plans of 31 May 1889, closed in June 1959, and the Dolphin, opened in 1854 under Mary Hill.

Bell Barn Road, cleared and partially renamed Rickman Drive when the Lee Bank estate was created, was originally developed post-1825. There was the Roebuck, and the Salmon (closed in 1939), the King's Head at 73, additions by William Naden in October 1878 and closed in 1914, and Chequers at 43 Bell Barn Lane, opened in 1835 and closed in 1924. There was the Queen's Arms at 212, dating from 1848 and updated to John Meggett's plans of 1879, which closed in May 1959. Its license was transferred to an intended pub at the corner of Fairfax and Edgehill Roads, West Heath. Then there was the Swan, at 88 Bell Barn Road. It opened in 1860, James Bryan was its first licensee. The Swan closed for the redevelopment of the area. Linking Bell Barn Road to Bath Row was Cregoe Street, also subject to redevelopment in the 1960s. The Falcon was closed in May 1922, the Warwick Arms closed in 1929. The Woodman, on the corner of Irving Street, opened in 1847, was taken over by M&B, and suffered the fate of the other pubs here. At 27 Upper Ryland Road was the Bell Barn Tavern, a Victorian beerhouse. It too closed for the building of the new estate. Linking Bristol Street and Lee Bank was Sun Street. The Royal Oak, on the corner with Bristol Street, faced St Luke's church. It was a beerhouse whose license was withdrawn in May 1922. The Malt Shovel in Sun Street was a Showell's Brewery house. W.J. Foulkes drew-up plans for its refurbishment on 26 July 1881. Further improvements were carried out according to the drawings of H.E. Twyford, on 26 November 1897. The Gough Arms at Sun Street West originated about 1840. It underwent modernisation from plans drawn-up by Henry Naden in May 1887. The Gough Arms closed in 1959 and its license was transferred to an intended pub to be built on the corner of Tile Cross Road and St Giles' Road, Sheldon.

Lee Bank Middleway, formerly Lee Bank Road, with some slight re-alignment, runs from Bristol Street almost up to Five Ways. The original pubs here dated from the 1830s. There was the British Queen, situated in a former Victorian terraced house, 52 Lee Bank Road, and set behind a small brick wall with iron railings. In its fore-garden were two close-cut trees, giving it an almost country-like atmosphere. The Dog & Partridge at 165, opened under licensee Thomas Lane in 1834. It was forced to close in 1941 under war-time restrictions. The Edgbaston Inn, later renamed the Edgbaston Tavern, was opened in 1840, Samuel Swann being its first licensee. By the 1920s the Edgbaston Hotel was opened nearby at 122 Lee Bank Road. Both houses went with the development of Lee Bank Middleway. The Old Thatched Cottage surrendered its beerhouse license to the Justices in January 1907. The tenant was paid a miserly £35 in compensation for his loss of livelihood.

The British Oak, another beerhouse, closed in 1930. The post-development replacement for these affectionately remembered locals was the Lee Tavern, an execrable one-storey concrete bunker construction for Davenport's (later taken over by M&B). Now demolished, it has left only a sour taste in the mouth, and the remembrance of man's inhumanity to man – it also served keg beer.

Wynn Street, now largely gone in the Lee Bank Development, formerly linked Bell Barn Road and Great Colmore Street. The Queen's Arms at 82 Wynn Street, opened by 1855, was hosted by landlord Samuel Hinley. The pub closed in 1959. Its license was transferred to the Cabin in Sheldon Heath Road. The White Swan, a Victorian beerhouse, closed in May 1922 as part of a general clearance under the 'fewer but better' scheme. The Three Crowns was cleared in the next purge in 1928.

Bow Street links Bristol Street and Holloway Head via Little Hill Street, later redeveloped as Irving Street. Along these two little roads were four pubs. The Half Moon was at 6 Little Hill Street. Stephen Dunn, who died in June 1796, was its first accredited licensee. He had been there since 1784. In 1864, William Beardmore took up the license and remained for thirty-eight years. During his tenure, in 1875 the street was extended and renamed Irving Street. Beardmore's widow, Sarah, saw the Half Moon's closure in 1915. The Bull's Head in Bow Street was a short-lived beerhouse under William Smith. It was there from 1841-1845. At 1 Bow Street, on the corner of Windmill Street, was the Wheatsheaf. It is first listed in the trade directory of 1828, with Joseph Ingram as licensee. In July 1884, architect Charles J. Hodson drew-up plans for its updating. The house was bought up by William Butler, and later became an M&B house. It closed in 1914. Fourteen years later the last pub-cum-beerhouse in Bow Street, the Hen & Chickens, also closed.

Holloway Head and Bath Row

Holloway Head, before the cutting of the Bristol Road, was the way to the West Country. The road leading from Smallbrook Street was Exeter Row, and Holloway Head was its extension. Here at the junction of the two roads was the Dog & Duck. It was a one-and-a-half-storey timber-framed house dating from the early seventeenth century, later encased in brick. Its first known licensee, in 1812, was Job Wiseman, though an indenture dating back to 1705 identifies Richard Danckes as an inn holder here. One incident to relate in connection with this house was an impromptu boxing match in 1821 between Phil Sampson, known as the 'Birmingham Youth', then a recruiting sergeant in the Warwickshire Militia, and Tom Hickman, alias the 'terrible gasman' of Dudley, one of the greatest blackguards associated with the sport. Hickman and his mates goaded the younger man into a fight. Much against expectations, Sampson was the victor. Hickman was hauled away to lick his wounds. The Dog & Duck was demolished in 1872, and a new much larger public house was built on the site. In 1890 the front was rebuilt to a restrained design by James & Lister Lea. This second pub closed in 1898.

A little further up the road was the Bowling Green, at No. 79. There had previously been an old timber-framed house on the site known as the Lord Wellington. It was pulled down in 1827 and replaced by an imposing three-storey brick-built house, built for licensee Ben Roden. Some years after, the Bowling Green was kept by Tom Hales, who added a dancing room to the pub. In 1854 the son of a former patron of the house, William Bragg, wrote of it:

The Dog & Duck, Holloway Head, 1860.

The original Bowling Green Inn, Holloway Head.

Above: *The Greyhound Inn, Holloway Head, 1964.*

Opposite above: *The Bowling Green, 1964.*

Opposite below: *The Unicorn, Holloway Head, 1960.*

The entrance to the house was by a broad, tiled hall, a little below the causeway. On the one side stood the kitchen, facing which was the bar parlour enclosed by a glass partition running nearly the length of the passage. The entrance to the smoking room was by a short passage down a flight of three oaken steps. Entering, you observed a dark panelled, oblong room, low ceiling, with a stuffed leather seat running completely around, save where it was broken by the door and fireplace. At equal distance arms were fixed, for the ease and comfort of the company, who regaled themselves with their churchwarden pipes and a jug of their favourite liquor.

In 1853 Mr Fitter was the host and in those days the smoking room was the nightly resort of a great many of the best householders in the neighbourhood, who came to hear, and talk over the news. Upon the table of this smoke room a brass box was standing upon four small legs was placed, containing tobacco. Whenever a customer wanted a pipeful, he placed a penny in a slot, which opened the lock and the lid of the box could be raised and a screw of tobacco extracted, and the lid relocked on closing it.

Whilst in the occupation of Mr Fitter, the dancing saloon on the green was unroofed during a severe storm. It was then removed to the old smoking room, which was raised level with the street and a drinking bar added. It is a notable fact that this addition to the 'Bowling Green' was the first place in Birmingham to which a music license was granted.

After the departure of Mr Fitter, the house was held for some years by a sporting landlord, Jack Littler, who transformed the dancing saloon and young sporting sparks often wagered heavily on the respective merits of their canine fancies, It was in the kitchen of this old inn that a noted dog fancier and rat catcher, 'Old Bluey', once backed himself to kill, with his teeth (his hands tied behind him), more rats in a given time than a famous terrier, and he won!

In the time of the next landlord, Mr Cooke, the old house was pulled down and a new and far more pretentious building took its place.

Around 1880 the Bowling Green issued tokens, but using the name the Observatory Inn. The token shows Chapman's windmill in its latter life, devoid of sails, when it was used as a camera obscura. It is not clear whether the windmill itself was selling beer, or whether it was used as an overflow from the Bowling Green. This old house was demolished, and a smaller premise, designed by Charles J. Hodson on 4 July 1883, was built on the site. It was taken over by Ansell's and became a tied house. The Bowling Green was closed in 1968, one of ten pubs later demolished in development areas around the city.

At 132 Holloway Head, on the corner of Speaking Stile Walk, was the Unicorn, an Ansell's tied house. Originally a beerhouse, it is shown on the Rating Maps for 1870. In 1951, licensee Leslie Collins purchased a full license at a cost of £1,800. This house was closed for the development of the Lee Bank estate. Across the other side of the road was the Greyhound at 89 Holloway Head. It was established as a beerhouse by Henry Guardner in 1835. Acquired by Beard's, it became a home-brew house, and continued brewing right up until 1965, making it the last home-brew house in the city. Under landlord John Hope the Greyhound was taken over by Bulmer's of Hereford and became a cider house. At one time it had the distinction of being the only public house in the West Midlands that did not sell beer. Extended in 1973 into the building next door, the Greyhound was later taken over by nearby Davenport's Brewery. The pub was renamed the Holloway. Following Davenport's takeover by Greenall Whitley, the house was sold off and converted to other uses.

Down the hill, and across the road from the Dog & Duck, was the Three Horseshoes, on the corner of Ellis Street. It was a Victorian beerhouse. On the corner of Marshall

Street was the Lamp Tavern. A beerhouse, it is shown on the Rating Maps of 1870. James Beaver carried out alterations to the Lamp from his plans drawn-up on 6 March 1878. These two old houses closed in May 1909. The White Swan, another old beerhouse now also gone, was updated by James & Lister Lea from their plans of 24 May 1891. A year earlier, in March 1890, architect Hiram Willcox updated the Duke of York nearby. At 48 Holloway Head was the Talbot, opened in 1897, under licensee William Moorfield. It closed in 1929, Mrs Annie Spinks was its last licensee. Following the completion of the Inner Ring Road, two tall tower blocks known as the Sentinels were built either side of the entrance to Holloway Head. Beneath one of them a pub, called the Sentinels, was built for Ansell's.

Just off Holloway Head are Blucher Street, Ellis Street, Gough Street and Washington Street. The Justice was situated at 49 Blucher Street, on the corner with Upper Gough Street. It was a beerhouse, shown on the 1870 Rating Maps. The house and licensee were paid compensation of £1,846 when the Justice was closed in 1912. Closed at the same time was the Dog & Partridge at 47 Ellis Street. It opened in 1839 with Samuel Chatwin as landlord, and was updated by little-known Birmingham architect William Carson on 22 November 1886. At 1 Gough Street was the Plough & Harrow, originating around 1828. It closed post-1842, but in the trade directory of 1849 there is an entry for the Plough & Harrow Revived, at 127½ Suffolk Street. Gough Street is barely a five-minute walk away, so there may be some connection between the two houses. There was a beerhouse

The Gough Arms, Marshall Street.

The Craven Arms, Gough Street.

called the Woodbine in Gough Street. It opened in 1897 as a William Butler tied house. It surrendered its license in January 1907. There was a beerhouse from the century before; the King's Head features in the obituary of licensee Edward Freeman, who died in March 1798. In Upper Gough Street was the St Thomas' Tavern, named after the church nearby. It was obliged to surrender its license on 31 December 1935, during a trawl of the city's pubs at this date in the 'fewer but better' scheme. Two pubs remain, the Gough Arms and the Craven Arms. The Gough Arms, now a free house, was formerly an Ansell's tied house. It is a rather bland inter-war pub, built on the site of an earlier house of the same name, dating from 1840. On the far corner, facing the Gough Arms, is the Craven Arms at

Detail from the Craven Arms.

1-2 Upper Gough Street. It is decorated in blue tiles, and above its corner entrance is an elaborate cartouche, advertising Holder's Ales, the brewery responsible for its construction. The pub has etched windows with ornate coloured glass above. Internally the house retains much of its Victorian origins. It was taken over by M&B in 1896, when it was described as a beerhouse in the sales catalogue. Some renovation occurred in 1906-7 from plans drawn-up by Arthur Edwards. The Gough Arms is now a Banks's house. In Washington Street was the Moulders Arms, a beerhouse that surrendered its license to the Justices in 1928.

Bath Row is the continuation of Holloway Head. Davenport's Brewery was located here until its closure by Greenall Whitley. Almost cheekily opposite was the Queen's Stores, an M&B house. It opened in 1928. Its first licensee was Wally Roberts. The Stores closed on 28 February 1962 and its license was transferred to the newly built Crusader at Five Ways. The Trees was a Kelsey's house, at 100 Bath Row at the junction with Wheeleys Lane. It first opened in 1853. Kelsey's rebuilt it in the early 1920s. Its architectural style was Egyptian; due to the discoveries of Howard Carter, all things Egyptian were very popular. This very pleasant public house closed in the 1960s when Bath Row was widened to link up with the Inner Ring Road. At 77 Bath Row was the New Cross Inn, opened in 1828, with William Braznor as landlord. In 1833 it changed its name to the Calthorpe Arms. It is shown and named on the 1870 Rating Maps. The house closed in 1884, George Yeates was its last landlord. Also shown on the Rating Maps was the Bird-in-Hand, a beerhouse. It was situated on the corner of Chequers Walk. At 153 Bath Row was the Beehive Inn. It was a late eighteenth-century two-storey house with recessed entranceway, allowing for a simple

The Glassmakers Arms, Holliday Street, 1962.

bench either side of the doorway. Above the central doorway was a homily painted on a semi-circular board:

> Within this hive we are all alive,
> Good liquor makes us funny,
> If you are dry step in and try,
> The flavour of our honey.

This old house was situated at the top of Bath Row, near Five Ways, on the corner with St Martin's Street. Likewise shown on the Rating Maps, it closed in 1913 for the development of Bath Row.

Just off Wheeleys Lane was Owen Street, now gone in the 1960s slum clearance. There was a beerhouse here called the Roller Arms. It surrendered its license to the Justices in May 1908. The licensee was paid a mere £10 in compensation. Adjoining Owen Street, and linking up to Bath Row, was Piggott Street. At No. 13 was the Britannia, originating in 1863. It was a Frederick Smith's tied house in 1937. Taken over by William Butler's Brewery in 1955, it closed in the 1960s for the development of the Lee Bank council estate. On the other side of Bath Row is a narrow little thoroughfare, linking up to Holliday Street. Its name is Communication Row. Here in the late 1820s was the Duke of Wellington. In 1855 its address changed to Holliday Street. It closed in 1893, Henry Bates was its last licensee.

Granville Street links Bath Row to Broad Street, crossing Holliday Street. It is a bit of a backwater now, but in its time possessed some interesting pubs. The New Inn on the corner of Granville Street and William Street was alternatively known as the 'Monkey House'. Legend has it that landlord John Hill kept a pet monkey who was allowed to wander freely around the pub. Developing a taste for beer, it had a habit of stealing customers' beer. One annoyed customer shut the monkey in an oven as a punishment, intending to release him after a few minutes, but forgot. True or not, it is on record that Arthur Hamblin carried out alterations to this beerhouse in 1889. The New Inn has now gone, replaced by Granville Square. Other beerhouses include the Globe, which surrendered it license in May 1909, the Bridge, which closed on 31 December 1935, and the Paviers Arms, updated by John Wilkinson from his plans of 29 August 1876, but now also demolished. There was the Royal Exchange; landlord Jack Cook advertised in a local newspaper in 1913 that he offered 'Noted Ales in fine condition'.

A detail of the splendid lamp and bracket on the Glassmakers Arms.

A beerhouse, it consisted of 'a roomy bar, cosy smoke room and a club room'. At 71-73 Holliday Street was the Elephant & Castle, a public house with a broad frontage onto the road. It opened in 1854 under John Pridmore, but alas is no more. Nearby at 77-79 Granville Street, on the corner of Holliday Street, was the Glassmakers Arms. It dated from 1850, with John Wilkinson as its first licensee. The house was taken over by Ansell's and they brought in architect William Jenkins to update their purchase. From his plans of 4 September 1882, he produced a pub lifted out of its back-street ordinariness by the refurbishment that he wrought. Its ground floor was opened up to give more light, its windows were given classical wooden columns spaced out every 4ft, and the windows themselves were leaded with stained-glass Art Nouveau designs. This friendly little back-street pub closed in 1968.

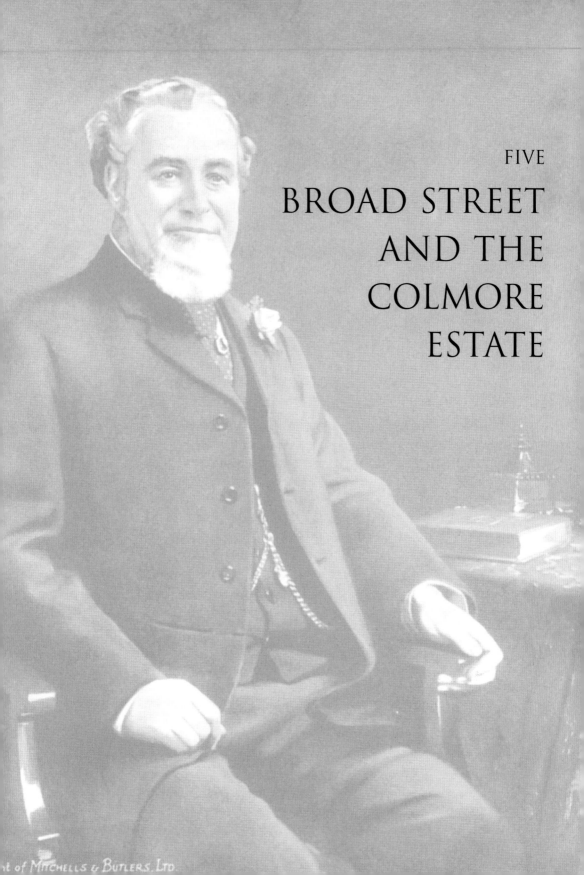

FIVE

BROAD STREET
AND THE
COLMORE
ESTATE

FIVE

BROAD STREET AND THE COLMORE ESTATE

Broad Street, for so long a backwater, blossomed in the 1990s following the opening of the International Convention Centre, the National Indoor Arena and the development of Brindley Place. Pubs, bars and bistros seemed to open overnight. Today it is a Mecca for the young, especially over the weekend. But everywhere that sells alcohol is not necessarily a public house. Basically if it is only open at night it is not a pub, and is therefore not included here.

Beginning from the city centre end of Broad Street, first taking the north side of the street, was a little beerhouse at 4-5 Broad Street, called the Royal Oak. It is shown on the Rating Maps of 1870. Its yard backed onto the old canal that used to exist here, roughly where Baskerville House is today. The area was cleared in the late 1920s for the development of the proposed Civic Centre. Now disappeared beneath the ICC was King Alfred Place. Here on the corner of Broad Street was the Compasses, a mid-Victorian pub, updated and refurbished by Robert Matthews from his plans of 28 June 1887. The Compasses closed in 1933.

At 26 Broad Street, on the corner of King Edward Place, was the original Crown, opened in 1781. The first proprietor of the Crown was Joseph Chatwin. Following his death in December 1784, his widow Mary took over. At the turn of the eighteenth century George Owen was licensee. During his tenancy, Mr Birt Davies, the Coroner, held many of his inquests here in lieu of a purpose-built Coroner's Court. William Butler from Leicestershire, later to become a founding partner in M&B, married George Owen's sister, Mary. On the day of their wedding they took possession of the London Works Tavern, a home-brew pub in Smethwick. In 1875 Butler became a partner with his brother-in-law in the Crown, and became manager on a day-to-day basis. Under him the Crown was reconstructed with its familiar clock turret and cupola, to the design of Bennetts Hill architect William Jenkins. While at Smethwick Butler had begun to brew for himself, and when the opportunity arose in 1880 to purchase twenty-five dwellings along King Edward Place, he did so. The buildings were demolished and Butler's Crown Brewery was built. From the start, Butler was able to brew 5,000 barrels a week, with storage for another 10,000, making it the largest storage in the Birmingham district. The Crown itself was reconstructed in 1883 by Jenkins,

112

The Crown Inn, Broad Street, 1928.

Left: *William Butler.*

Below: *The Brass House, Broad Street, and beyond it the Crown Inn.*

and updated in 1930 by E.F. Reynolds, who did the ground floor with rusticated piers, parapet and new domed clock tower. The pub came under threat in 1984 with the construction of the ICC, with the daft idea that this then listed building should be jacked up onto rails and moved to its intended site next to the Brasshouse. It was estimated that this little move would cost between £600,000 and £800,000. Common sense prevailed and the ICC was built around the Crown. Amidst threats of court proceedings over M&B's extensive renovations in the 1990s, including the removal of a gable wall, when no permission had been given, the Crown, minus its original character (and a number of walls), has survived. The Brasshouse, as previously mentioned, was a £1¼ million conversion by Ansell's of an old brassworks, dating back to 1780. Situated next door to the ICC this was the acknowledged flagship of the company in Birmingham. The emphasis was on creating 'a meeting place for both local and foreign businessmen', as the advertising hype announced. On the first floor the brewery built a restaurant. The Brasshouse was opened on 14 December 1988 by Ansell's Managing Director, Tony Hales.

The Prince of Wales Stores, situated near the theatre of the same name, destroyed during the Blitz, opened in 1869 under James Rodgers. Nearby on the corner of Cumberland Street was another beerhouse, the New Inn, shown on the Rating Plans of 1870. The Roebuck at 108 Broad Street, was on the corner with Ryland Street. It originated around 1839 under the appropriately named landlord, Roe Butler, and was closed in 1966 at the time of the redevelopment of Five Ways. Not far away was the Broad Street Tavern at 88 Broad Street. It was a beerhouse, shown on the Rating Maps of 1870. William Jenkins, architect of the Crown updates, carried out alterations to the Tavern from his plans of 26 November 1880. The New Inns closed in 1924. W.S. Seamark had undertaken updating to this beerhouse from his plans of 5 April 1894. On the corner of Ruston Street was the Victoria, at No. 75. It opened in 1869, closing a century later for the redevelopment of Five Ways. Up on the corner of Ladywood Road was the Five Ways Inn. Originally known as the Five Ways Tavern, it originated around 1834 under licensee John Pritchett. Taken over by M&B in the 1890s, the old house was demolished an d a new one built. This proved to be a large three-storey house at a prominent entrance to central Birmingham. Above its main corner entrance, in large letters, covering the first and second floors, was written 'Mitchells and Butlers Good Honest Beer'. Obviously a concern here by the brewers for the short-sighted. Architect Alfred Reading was responsible for the build, from his plans of 15 March 1893. The Five Ways Inn closed on 29 May 1967 for the construction of the Middle Ring Road.

Starting on the other side of Broad Street from the city centre was the Night 'N' Day, a Courage house dating from the early 1970s. It was set down in a concrete underpass, with full-length plate-glass windows enabling you to see the concrete outside. Its one saving grace was that it sold Imperial Russian Stout. Up near the corner of Gas Street are two 1990s pubs, the Merchant Stores and the Walkabout Inn. Both are conversions of former Victorian commercial premises. The Rat & Parrot, another of the new boys, is more a café-bar. It opened in November 1998. Opening in November 2002, the Figure of Eight is a Weatherspoon's pub. Originally it was to have been called the Salaman Cutler, taking its name from a partner in a local glassmaking company. The pub is a conversion of a 1932 art deco building by Bernard G. Warr, originally used as a car showroom, and latterly as the offices of the National Cash Register Co. Ltd. On the corner of Granville Street stands O'Neils of Broad Street. It began life as the Granville, an M&B house, built in 1923. The architect was Arthur Edwards, and the house was built in the Jacobean style, so popular in the 1920s.

The Granville, corner of Broad Street and Granville Street, 1964.

The pub was renamed the Westward Ho in 1963, but reverted back to the Granville in 1986. In 1995 it changed its name once again, and became O'Neill's, a cod-Irish theme pub. This brought it into dispute with a real Irish pub, Mick O'Neill's house of the same name in Curzon Street. A compromise was reached, and 'of Broad Street' was added. Two more Irish theme pubs, Waxy O'Connor's and Brannigan's, are situated up near Five Ways. Brannigan's was opened by First Leisure in 1998, in the former Maples furniture store. Apparently it cost £2 million to purchase and convert the building. Waxy O'Connor's opened in 2001. Curiously, and heavens knows why, there is a beech tree that grows from the ground floor up to balcony level. Better to have concentrated on a better selection of beer one would have thought. On the corner of Gas Street is another 1990s pub, B2SIXTY. It is a ground-floor conversion of the 1960s Stanway House, former Midlands headquarters of British Rail. More nightclub than public house is Studi Bakers and Tiger Tiger, its name written in letters 6ft high – again presumably for the short-sighted. It offers 'six distinct environments', as the add-boys promoted it.

Of the beerhouses along Broad Street, there was the Queen's Arms, which was closed down by the Justices in May 1922, as was the King's Arms; the White Hart, at 57 Broad Street, opened in 1854, and closed in 1926; The Board, at 199 Broad Street, which opened in 1880 and the Victoria Tavern, updated by William Jenkins in February 1888, are both now gone. At 157 Broad Street was an un-named beerhouse, also updated by Jenkins from his plans of 2 March 1891.

The Tap & Spile and Merchant Stores, viewed from Gas Street basin.

Leading off from Broad Street on its south side was the Malt Shovel in Fordrove Street. It opened in 1791 under John Taylor, closing with the expansion of the Goods Yard extension of New Street Station. In Wharf Street, an 'L'-shaped road linking Broad Street and Suffolk Street, were a number of pubs. At 31 was the Queen's Arms, just six doors up from the Navigation at 35-6 Wharf Street, on the corner of Bridge Street. It dated from 1823. From 1855 until its closure in 1881, William Wright was its long-serving licensee. At 36a Wharf Street was the Anchor, a beerhouse situated almost opposite the Navigation, as is shown on the Rating Plans of 1870. The Bull's Head at No. 37 originated pre-1812. It closed seventy years later. The George & Dragon at 47 originated about the same time, and closed more or less about the same time, in 1886 for the cutting of Holliday Street.

In Bridge Street, where Cadbury's had a factory, stood the Victoria. Established in 1838, it had apparently closed by 1848. The next road along is Gas Street. Here was situated the Navigation Inn of 1860. This house came up for sale in November 1900, but was sold as:

A Freehold Property comprising the Retail Shop and Dwelling House, until recently known as the NAVIGATION INN.

Of replacements there have been three. The Tap & Spile is a pleasing conversion of an early nineteenth-century office and warehouse on three levels, with access from the canal; the James Brindley is on the Gas Street canal basin, and the Glass House is another partially renovated warehouse conversion. In Granville Street was the Exchange, a beerhouse closed under the 'fewer but better' scheme in 1929. Nearby Tennant Street runs parallel to Broad Street. At No. 99 was the Vyse Arms, which opened in 1839, closed in 1850 and re-opened as the Exhibition in 1851. By 1854 it had become the Exhibition Gin Palace. It closed in 1873. The Crown & Barrel was a beerhouse dating from 1870, and is shown on the Rating Maps, as was the Bellevue Inn at 165, dating from 1862. Also appearing on the 1870 Map was the Fountain Tavern, at 178 Tennant Street. Finally the Black Horse, it originated in 1861 under licensee William Tew. All the houses here have now gone.

In William Street were two James & Lister Lea-designed houses, the King's Arms of 1901, for M&B, and the Roebuck, also of 1901, for Ansell's. They were very similar in style, built on street corners in red brick and terracotta, with short towers above their corner entrances. Both regrettably are now gone. The original King's Arms dated from 1823, the Roebuck was even earlier; built on a 100-year lease dated from 25 March 1793. There were two more public houses here, the White Horse, at 98 William Street, which dated from 1840 and closed in 1969, and the British Oak, shown on the 1870 Rating Maps. Just off Broad Street at Five Ways is St Martin's Street, part of the 1820s development by the Rector of St Martin's, known as Islington. At 33 St Martin's Street was the Dog, a beerhouse shown on the Rating Maps. It originated in 1861. The Red Lion was at No. 61 and dated from 1820. Thomas Wheeler was the last licensee when this house closed in 1902. Of an unknown address in the lane was the Wheatsheaf. Joseph Hoe was listed as landlord in the directory of 1825. The house, for whatever reason, had closed by 1830. On the corner of Bishopgate Street and Tennant Street is the City Tavern, a Highgate Brewery tied house. It began life as the Bull's Head in 1788. In 1899 M&B bought the house, negotiated a new lease, and commissioned James & Lister Lea to design a new house. A little over the top perhaps, even for the Leas the building is perhaps a little bit too fussy. Nonetheless it is now a Grade II-listed house. Regrettably, due to planning blight, it suffered a loss in trade, and was closed down in July 1998. Unprotected as it then was, M&B simply looking for compensation, thieves broke in and stole its beautiful carved mahogany bar and stained-glass snob screens. Rescued by Walsall-based Highgate Brewery, £600,000 was spent in refurbishment, and the house re-opened as the City Tavern in November 2001. Other pubs here include the Islington Stores, opened on 25 March 1788 on a 100-year lease. The Lamp at No. 64, shown on the 1870 Rating Plans, and the Freemasons Arms, an 1880s beerhouse.

Up at Five Ways, just around the corner from Broad Street, is Islington Row. At 23 Islington Row was the Islington Tea Gardens. Established by 1818, at that time it would have been very pleasantly situated on the edge of the countryside. A little earlier in 1812, it had been known as the Islington Cottage. This pub with gardens closed in 1853-4. The Anchor at 33 Islington Row was on the corner of Tennant Street. It was a substantial early nineteenth-century house, rebuilt in February 1881 to the drawings of William Jenkins, and taken over by M&B in 1891. It was forced to close on 16 April 1961 for the reconstruction of the Five Ways area, and the development of a new shopping centre. The White Swan was at 81 Islington Row. It dated back to 1812. Pub architects James & Lister Lea updated, rather than rebuilt, it for landlord John Watts in May 1891. The lease of the house expired in the summer of 1908. There was also a beerhouse here called the Swan. It was opened by William Johns in 1869. Alterations and updates were carried out to the designs of A&J Henwood in 1882. The Crusader opened on 1 August 1963 as part of the Five Ways Shopping Centre. It was built to replace the demolished Anchor, whose license it was given. An M&B house, very similar in style to the 1960s Bull Ring pubs, it still survives, but given the close proximity of the City Tavern, it would not perhaps be your first choice.

Ladywood Lane, now Ladywood Middleway, forms the natural western border of the town centre. At 24 Ladywood Lane, on the corner of Grosvenor Street West, was the

Station Inn, named after Five Ways Station, barely five minutes walk away. It originated in 1870, and was later taken over by Ansell's. The pub was forced to close because of war-time restrictions in 1941. Also closed about this time was the Turk's Head, at 53. It originated in 1854, and was closed in 1940. At 70 Ladywood Lane was the Eagle & Ball, opened in 1854 and closed in 1961. The Squirrel, along Ladywood Middleway, was an estate pub built after the Ladywood slum clearance of the 1960s. It is an Ansell's house, the name is taken from the Ansell's squirrel motif. The London design boys excelled themselves with inanity here: they placed a tree in the middle of the Acorn lounge. Why? is the obvious question. Moving back towards the town centre we come to Ruston Street. On the corner of Ruston Street and Rawlins Street was the Vine Inn, opened in 1853 and closed in 1974. The Cup at No. 12 was a beerhouse shown on the 1870 Rating Maps, and the Waggon & Horses, at the junction of Grosvenor Street West, was there between 1841 and 1871. Architects Wood & Kendrick, who designed the White Horse in Congreve Street, updated the Slaters Arms at 38 Ruston Street in 1895. This house was closed on 30 January 1926, during one of the Licensing Justices periodic purges of back-street pubs. The Lamp at 51, opened by 1887, had closed by 1899, and the New Inn and the Orange Tree are both shown on the Rating Maps. The Orange Tree closed in 1901.

Ryland Street, the next road along, had five pubs or beerhouses in the period from 1840 to 1962. The Rose & Crown was there by 1861 and closed in 1936. The Ryland Arms at 33-5 Ryland Street was an M&B pub. H.W. Hobbis, architect of the Antelope in Sparkhill, undertook renovations here in 1935. This house was closed on 20 May 1962 and demolished in the slum clearances of Ladywood. The Grapes, a Victorian beerhouse, was also demolished then. The Rutland Arms, at 1 Upper Ryland Road, was there during the 1860s, as was the Grand Turk, closed by the Justices in 1913. In Essington Street, linking Ryland Street and Sheepcote Street, was the Royal Oak, a beerhouse closed by the Justices in 1913. The licensee got just £190 for loss of earnings.

Grosvenor Street West links up with Ryland Street. At No 1 was the Grosvenor Arms of 1840, closed in 1914. The Colmore Arms, a beerhouse, shown on the 1870 Rating Maps, was referred for closure in 1913. The White Swan at 110 Grosvenor Street West was established by William Griffiths in 1869. It was taken over by Rushton's Brewery of Aston, and in 1924 became an Ansell's house. The pub was updated during the 1930s and given an art deco frontage. The house survived the slum clearance of the street and in the 1990s was 'restored' as a Victorian public house by the brewers. Across the road at 111, and now long gone, was the Royal Oak, a Victorian beerhouse. On the corner of Sherborne Street was the Sherborne Tavern, of 1854, which surrendered its license in May 1909. In nearby Sheepcote Street, at No. 1 was the Board, a beerhouse listed in 1849. At 2 was the Islington Vaults of 1854, closed in 1924. At 8 was the Green Dragon, dating from 1828, and surviving until 1903. Nearby was the Islington Tavern, later renamed the Islington Racquet Court, when a tennis court was added out the back in 1853. The pub was closed by the Justices in 1913. The Pheasant, a beerhouse, was at No. 41 between 1870 and 1888 at least. Further along the road was the Cottage of Content, dating from the 1840s, and closed by 1884. The Albion, another beerhouse, appears on the 1870 Plans. It was taken over by M&B, and closed during the 1960s slum clearances. There was one significant replacement for the loss of the above public houses, that was the Fiddle & Bone. It was opened on 18 June 1997 by Danny Longstaff and Mark Robinson of the City of Birmingham Symphony Orchestra. The pub's name relates to musical instruments – the violin and trombone. It was a musical pub with live music, ranging from classical to jazz to folk. Following a dispute with nearby neighbours over noise, the pub was forced to close in March 2003.

The former Three Horse Shoes, St Peter's Place, 1935.

Cumberland Street had the Beehive, at No. 18. A beerhouse, it was there by 1870, but lost its license in January 1907. Leading off from there is the mysteriously named Oozells Street. There were two beerhouses, both shown on the 1870 Rating Maps, and both now gone, the Forge Tavern at No. 8, and the White Lion, updated by H.J. Greatrex from his plans of 2 October 1890. At Oozells Street North was the Eagle, in existence by 1848. It closed in 1940, Mrs Myrtle Gilson being its last licensee. Brasshouse Passage was cleared in the 1980s for the construction of the ICC. It ran alongside the present Brasshouse pub. In 1870, a beerhouse, the Britannia, is clearly shown on the Rating Plans. Also gone beneath the ICC are two little streets, St Peter's Place and St Martin's Place. At their junction at Broad Street was the Three Horse Shoes. It was a mock-Tudor, half-timbered house, built in 1817 and converted into a pub in 1867. Alterations were carried out to the Shoes by architect Pritchard Davis, from his plans of 2 November 1876. Of morbid interest was the fact that a boastful man drinking here said that he could withstand any blow to his chest. Of course he was killed by a fatal blow. The house later surrendered its license to the Justices in May

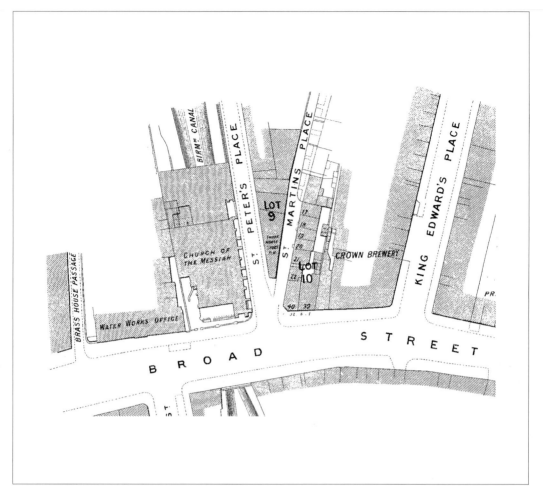

From the sales details, the Three Horse Shoes, 1894.

1908. It changed its use a number of times before demolition, including its final incarnation as an antique shop.

Either side of the old Bingley Hall, now gone, were King Edward's Place and King Alfred's Place. At 16 King Edward's Place was the Exhibition, opened in 1888. It was one of the twenty-four houses bought up by William Butler, and demolished for the expansion of the Crown Brewery. The Bingley Tavern at 14-16 King Alfred's Place was a post-1850s house. By 1884 it had become the Bingley Hall Hotel. Its site now lies beneath the Convention Centre.

Bingley Hall backed onto Cambridge Street. At 5 Cambridge Street was the Baskerville Tavern, named after printer John Baskerville who lived nearby in the eighteenth century. The Tavern was opened in 1887, with John Gaunt as landlord. It closed in 1901, and the site was cleared in the 1920s for the construction of what was to become Baskerville House. At 23 was the Hand & Bottle, a canal-side pub. It opened in 1859 under John Brookes. He was followed by William Payne, its second and last publican. The house closed in 1874.

Above: *The Prince of Wales, Cambridge Street.*

Opposite above: *The Longboat, c. 1969.*

Opposite below: *The Malt House, King Edward's Road.*

Above *The Shakespeare, Summer Row.*

Opposite: *The Cambridge Inn, Cambridge Street, 1928.*

The Prince of Wales was originally an un-named beerhouse at 84 Cambridge Street. It was taken over by the Holt Brewery, and its ground floor rebuilt. In the rear lounge until its 1990s 'refurbishment' was a beautiful etched window depicting the brewery's squirrel trademark, one of only two then left in the city. In 1934 the Prince became an Ansell's tied house. It has featured in CAMRA'a Good Beer Guide virtually from 1975 until the present day, due largely to its long-time licensees, Paddy and Nancy McCarthy. With Nancy's departure the pub was gutted, and the etched window 'removed'. One hundred yards or so down the road, and set back off the road, is the Malt House, where US President Bill Clinton famously sat on the outside balcony to drink a pint while attending the G8 Conference in Birmingham. Across on the other side of the road in the Crescent was the Crescent Tavern, a short-lived public house dating from 1841 to 1852. Just off nearby Kingston Row, built along the canal, is the Longboat, an Ansell's pub, opened in February 1970. The name is a misnomer, and more correctly should have been the Narrow Boat, the proper name for what the uninitiated call a barge. During the 1980s it developed a lethargy, but was taken over by the

Firkin chain. With the break-up of Firkin it has again entered the doldrums. It is a good pub, in a good location, looking for direction. The Longboat's license was transferred from the Cambridge Inn, when it closed in the late 1960s. The pub, on the corner of Cambridge Street and Crescent Wharf, dated from 1875.

Summer Row is off Cambridge Street. Of the various pubs opened here, only one remains, the Shakespeare. It was originally a beerhouse on the corner with Lionel Street. In existence by 1870, it was taken over by M&B in 1892, gaining a full license in the process. In the following year James & Lister Lea were brought in to design a new pub on the site. The pub they created was subdued in comparison to their normal houses. It is a three-storey public house, built in red brick, with not even a suggestion of terracotta; decidedly Gothic in style, with arched windows to the ground floor, a corner entrance, all topped off with the suggestion of a tower into the roof, with a cockerel weather vane above that. It went through a quiet period in the 1970s and '80s, but emerged at the end of the century as a vibrant lunch-time venue. Inside it has still retained some particularly fine features, including its original Victorian bar-back. At 17 Summer Row was the White Swan, opened in 1817 under John Tilsley. It was altered by architect Edward Sims in June 1877, and in 1883 William Jenkins oversaw further changes. Bought up by brewer Henry Mitchell, it was rebuilt as an M&B house to the designs of the Leas in January 1894. The White Swan closed in 1933. Five doors up from the White Swan was the Rose & Crown at 12 Summer Row. It was established in 1820 by wood turner John Bradshaw. With the expiry of its lease in 1895, the house was closed, and the site was redeveloped. Very briefly from 1860 to 1863 the Wine & Spirits Vaults was at 20 Summer Row. Three doors up from the corner of Charlotte Street was the Board Vaults, established as early as 1810 and closed upon the expiry of its 100-year lease. The King William, a little beerhouse at 32, was there pre-1870, but gone by 1890. Almost opposite Lionel Street was the Waggon & Horses at 39 Summer Row. Dating from pre-1827, it was closed by the Justices as part of their 'fewer but better' scheme in 1919. The Fisherman's Arms at 49 was opened in 1887. It closed in 1894. The Green Man, a beerhouse, was at 141 in 1865, but gone by 1870. The Jolly Spade Maker (and why shouldn't they be jolly?) is briefly mentioned in the trade directory of 1818, with George Bradshaw as licensee. Of the same date was the Friday Bridge Inn, under Zachariah Slaney. Both had disappeared by the 1830s.

The Parade is the continuation of Summer Row. There was the Apple Tree, a beerhouse, that surrendered its license in 1907; the Navigation at 1 Parade originated in 1818 and closed down for road widening during the 1970s; the Havannah, a beerhouse, closed in 1918; and the Burton Stores at 49 Parade. It was a Victorian house, with a 1920s added mock-Tudor front. This pub closed in 1965 for the redevelopment of Paradise Circus. The King Edward VI, at 17 Parade, was another old house, dating from 1834. It was renovated by William Sapcote & Son in 1880, taken over by M&B a decade later, and closed in 1995. The site is now occupied by a car showroom. At the bottom of the hill, turning right, is George Street and the Colmore estate. At 62 George Street was the Newhall Hill Tavern. It dated from around 1850 and closed in 1877, when its lease fell due. Further up the hill was the Smiths' Inn, a Victorian beerhouse compulsorily closed by the Justices in 1918. In Holland Street, just off George Street, was the Green Man of 1850-53. At the bottom of the road is Charlotte Street. At 18 was the Why Not, a beerhouse that surrendered it license in May 1908. At 50 Charlotte Street was the Warwick Arms of 1870, and on the corner of Holland Street itself was the Hope & Anchor. It opened in 1805. By 1852 its address turned the corner and became 14 Holland Street. In 1918 the Justices revoked its license and

The Jam House, formerly The Square, St Paul's Square.

Joseph Mobley proved to be its last landlord. The top end of Newhall Street, near St Paul's church, was once known as Mount Street. At 2 Mount Street, later 186 Newhall Street, was the Duke of Marlborough. It was a mid-eighteenth-century house of four rooms with a central entrance. John Hodgkins was licensee during the 1780s. William Jenkins carried out updates and refurbishment in 1882. A decade later, brewers Davenport's made it a tied house. The Duke closed in 1918. At 13 Mount Street, later 191-3 Newhall Street, was the Star, an imposing three-storey Georgian house built around 1765, with a pillared central door and a high bay window to the right. During the 1860s it became the Star Hotel & Family Boarding House. It closed in 1918, and was converted into an office, with workshops to the rear. The Golden Cup was at 36 Mount Street. Only one licensee is known for definite, Job Steward, in 1828. A beerhouse, the Beehive, appears on the 1870 Rating Maps. It was three doors up from Charlotte Street. At 174-176 Mount Street was the Turk's Head, dating from 1796 under licensee Thomas Southall. The license was temporarily surrendered to the Justices in 1892, but was then re-issued on an annual basis up to 1919.

The Rope Walk, St Paul's Square.

In Mary Ann Street, that little street that links St Paul's Square and Livery Street, was the French Horn, a licensed victuallers, supplying lunches and beer for the Jewellery Quarter workers. It opened as early as 1818 under licensee Sarah Brittle. One hundred years later the French Horn was recommended for closure. Samuel Holmes was its last licensee. In St Paul's Square itself are two pubs, the Square, a somewhat upmarket establishment with a bar and restaurant, and the Rope Walk, a Banks' house, that opened in May 1989 at a cost of £1.5 million. Both are of interest in their own ways. They replaced a much earlier pub in the Square, the Britannia of 1810, now long gone. In 1876 it changed its name to the Britannia Inn to distinguish it from the later built Britannia in nearby Cox Street. Also in Cox Street at No. 10 was the Roebuck, of 1828, under Ben Robatham. This house closed in 1893.

Linking Livery Street to Constitution Hill is the drab Henrietta Street, home of two Victorian public houses, the Leopard of 1840-55, and the Glasscutters' Arms of 1834. There was also a beerhouse, the Bunch of Grapes, run by button maker John Malpass, who died in February 1806. Nearby in Fleet Street was the St Paul's Chapel, at No. 37. In existence by 1808, it closed in 1892; the Green Man at No. 23 opened pre-1790 and closed a century

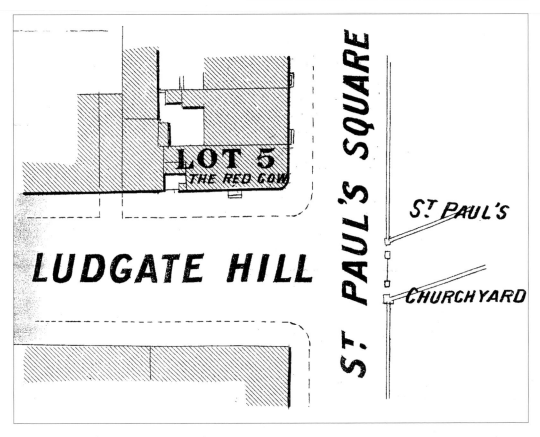

Sales notice for the Red Cow, 23 October 1894.

later in 1892 under the same Improvement Scheme that closed the Chapel. Finally the Fox, later the Old Fox, at 14 Fleet Street. It had opened by 1825 and was likewise closed in 1892. Water Street, the other side of Ludgate Hill, competing in drabness with Henrietta Street, and nearly winning, had five public houses over the years. The Challenge was at 2 Water Street; it opened in 1901 under Arthur Cutler and closed in 1930 under licensee Walter Plaskett. The Swan was at 34 Water Street, 1853 to 1882; the Bull's Head, also at 34 (but at a later date, following street renumbering), was there from 1841 to post-1882. The Coach & Horses is listed in the directory of 1818 when Sarah Griffin was licensee; and then there was the Waterloo Tavern, of post-1815, which closed in 1840.

Ludgate Hill, the approach road to St Paul's Square, has two public houses now, where formerly there were four. The Red Cow was a beerhouse on the corner with St Paul's Square. Offered for sale in October 1894, it was described as 'well-known as a house of very good business'. At 40 Ludgate Hill, and not to be confused with the pub of the same name in Church Street, was the Roebuck. It opened in 1828, or thereabouts, with Thomas Morris as landlord. It was obliged to surrender its license in 1914. The Grand Turk, a late eighteenth-century public house, was noted for the fact that inquests were held here up to January 1878. There is a story of how Birmingham's first Coroner, Dr Birt-Davies, when summing up a case, was interrupted by a loud noise at the back of the room.

Sitting on a bagatelle table were two reporters, one of whom got up, the weight of the other still sitting tipped up the heavy wooden cover, precipitating him onto the floor, along with balls, cues and frame, creating a very loud noise. Birt-Davies, believing the reporter to be drunk (it was a pub after all), ordered the arrest of the offending person, and promptly sentenced him to seven days in Winson Green Prison for contempt of court. Only later did the landlord explain the circumstances, and Birt-Davies, mellowed by a brandy and water, withdrew the sentence. The first licensee of the Grand Turk, in 1796, was John James, landlord until 1818. The license of the house was withdrawn in 1891 and the Grand Turk was demolished for road widening. Upon completion the house was rebuilt, and its license restored. It finally closed in 1900. St Paul's Tavern, at 24 Ludgate Hill, opened in 1860, with George Heeley as its first landlord. This old beerhouse was taken over by M&B, and obtained a full license in 1918. It had a delightful front bar where you could sit and watch the world go by as you supped your pint. It also had a smoke room in the back, that gave the impression of being the 'best room', reserved for aunties and special visitors. The Tavern was

The Mongolian, Ludgate Hill.

The Actress & Bishop, Ludgate Hill.

extended sideways in the 1980s, creating a large serving area with no atmosphere whatsoever. As often as not the front bar was locked after that, and the Tavern's regulars moved on. In the late 1990s this much-loved little pub was converted into the Mongolian Bar and next door its extension became the Xanadu Bar, specialising in Mongolian barbecues. Why? What is the purpose? Luckily what has been done can be undone, under a sympathetic new owner. Immediately across the road is the Actress & Bishop, a very good conversion of a former Victorian commercial premises. Opened in the 1990s it offers real ale downstairs, and live music upstairs in an intimate atmosphere.

Finally Lionel Street and its pubs, and this survey of the Colmore estate west of Great Charles Street Queensway is complete. The area within the Inner Ring Road was surveyed in volume one. At 39 Lionel Street was the Son of Mirth, a public house opened in 1860 with Joseph Ingram as its first landlord. It had closed by 1862, without even a chuckle. A century earlier, in 1760, Joseph Aston opened the Fox & Dogs at 46 Lionel Street. The house surrendered its license in 1860, when the leases on properties here fell due, but, following rebuilding, the license was restored by the Justices and was renewed up to 1896. Alfred John Harris was its last landlord. The Golden Lion opened in 1818. In 1893 it was demolished for road widening. The rebuilt house, designed by James & Lister Lea, had its license restored, and continued to serve ale up to 1918. It closed as a Holt's tied house. The Pig & Whistle, a three-storey house conversion on the Colmore estate, was at 138 Lionel Street. It is first listed in the trade directory of 1828. Piercy Knight was its first licensee. In 1830 he renamed the house the King's Arms. In 1839 followed the accession of Queen Victoria, and the house was renamed the Queen's Arms, under licensee John Lancaster. The house closed in 1855. There were four beerhouses along this road. The Plough & Harrow opened around 1799, Edward Wilding being its first licensee. It closed in 1818. The Leopold and the Highland Laddie, both early nineteenth-century houses, were closed under an Improvement Scheme in 1892. The Rose survived a little longer, it was closed as part of the 'fewer but better' scheme of the Licensing Justices, in 1918. The Antelope was at 56 Bread Street, now the eastern end of Lionel Street between Newhall Street and Livery Street. The pub took its name from the Royal Warwickshire Regiment, whose cap badge was an antelope. The pub was in existence by 1823, and closed in 1890.

GOSTA GREEN AND THE JENNENS ESTATE

SIX

GOSTA GREEN AND THE JENNENS ESTATE

Gosta Green

Gosta Green was once an open common covered with grass and gorse, hence its original name of Gorsey Green. It was known as Gorsty Green by 1677, and is shown as Gosty Green on Thomas Hanson's Plan of Birmingham for 1785. Nowadays much of it has disappeared beneath Aston University campus.

Lancaster Street, near the Central Fire Station, was originally known as Walmer Lane. As a street it dated back to pre-1553. Back in 1767 John Overton was landlord of the Lamp in Walmer Lane. Also in this old street was the Queen's Head, of 1828, under William Terry, and the White Lion, the obituary of whose licensee, Robert Ruston, appears in the Birmingham *Gazette* for 4 October 1804. With the change in name of the street, it was also given street numbers. At 9 Lancaster Street, from 1820, was the Green Man. It was closed and demolished in 1900 for the final stage of the cutting of Corporation Street. At 16 Lancaster Street was the Shakespeare's Head, a beerhouse which surrendered its license in 1883. At 19 was the Britannia, under John Cutler during the 1840s. The City Arms was at 20 Lancaster Street, and opened in 1900 with Edgar Evans as licensee. The house appears in an advertisement in the *Birmingham Echo* for 11 October 1913:

> ELI SIMCOX, The City Arms, Lancaster Street (50 yards from Corporation Street). Late of the Beehive, Bull Street, for twenty years. Home-Brewed Ales on tap in sparkling condition. Fully Licensed. Grand Oak Panelled Billiard Room, Private entrance. Large Club Room to let free. Extensive Bars. Well upholstered Smoke Rooms. Buffet Bar. Snacks always ready. A hearty welcome to all.

Less than two years later though the City Tavern was closed when this busy traffic junction was redeveloped to ease traffic congestion.

The present Turk's Head is a 1960s pub, built on the site of a much earlier house dating back to 1812. The Red Lion, at 31 Lancaster Street dating from the same year, temporarily lost its license in 1883. William Jenkins was called in to design a new pub on 26 November

1889. The house was closed in 1901 for street improvements. At 38 was the Alhambra Palace which, though it possessed an exotic name, was no more than a beerhouse, in existence by 1861 with Bridget Murray as landlady. The Brunswick Hotel, on the corner of Lench Street, was a Cheshire's Brewery tied house, later taken over by M&B. Victorian in origin, it closed on 14 January 1967 and was demolished for the construction of Lancaster Circus. At 56 Lancaster Street was the White Lion, which dated from 1815. It closed in 1930. The Brass Guns Inn was a little beerhouse at 61 Lancaster Street, on the edge of the Gun Quarter. Architect Thomas Hill designed a new ground-floor front for this old Georgian house on 12 September 1882. Its name was changed to the Cross Guns in 1883, and the house continued until road widening brought about its demolition in 1902. The Green Dragon, later renamed the George & Dragon, originated post-1825, and was closed for redevelopment in 1890. Three more beerhouses: the Apple Tree was updated by J.E. Webb from his plans of 9 December 1899, the curiously named Straw Pit was updated by William Jenkins from his plans of 17 November 1892, and the Manchester Tavern was updated by architect Franklin Cross on 8 September 1887.

Brickiln Street, another road now gone, was just off Lancaster Street. It was cut pre-1781. There was a beerhouse here called Chequers, listed in the directories in the late 1820s. At 17 Brickiln Street was the White House, which originated around 1815 and was abandoned under the Improvement Scheme of 1882. The White Swan was in existence by 1860; James Bryan was licensee. Legge Street, which links Corporation Street to Gosta Green, has largely now gone. At 57 was the Oscott Stores, a beerhouse. It surrendered its license in 1883. The White Swan at 85 Legge Street dated from 1800. Its first known licensee was Sarah Farmer. The White Swan closed in 1957 for rebuilding work along the northern edge of Corporation Street, at its junction with the Aston Road. The Britannia, on the corner of Aston Road, opened in 1812. Its license was temporarily suspended in 1883 under the Improvement Scheme, but was restored the year after. The Britannia closed in 1930. Just at the start of the Aston Road, at No. 8, was the Green Man. It is referred to in an advertisement in *Aris's Gazette* for 1800, where it was offering its services as a livery. The house closed in 1868.

Staniforth Road overlooks Aston University. At the junction with Corporation Street is the King Edward VII, designed for M&B by the architectural firm of Wood & Kendrick in 1904, and opened in the following year. Built in red brick and buff terracotta, with a clock tower above its corner entrance, it is perhaps a little subdued in its English Classical style when compared with the more vibrant house style of James & Lister Lea. The house was renamed the Ben Jonson in 1976. Its Edwardian features were ripped out, to be replaced by mock beams and rough plaster work, the like of which if carried out by a Tudor plasterer would have seen him thrown out of his guild. With the building of the flyover nearby, the building became isolated and lost trade. It was given a new daft name, and began to sell draught cider to attract the students across the road, but somehow this scheme did not succeed and the pub closed. For a number of years the house was derelict and boarded up, while its clock was stolen. But at the turn of the Millennium, with new owners, it has been given a new lease of life as a free house. Not too far away was the Black Boy at 32 Staniforth Street. It was established around 1825, closed temporarily in 1883, but had its license restored the following year. It was taken over by Holt's, but closed again in 1906. The Bull's Head was a beerhouse. Its license was abandoned under the Improvement Scheme of 1879. The Queen's Head, another beerhouse, had its license withdrawn in 1926. Linking Lancaster Street to Staniforth Street was Canal Street, a narrow little thoroughfare now lost to redevelopment.

The King Edward VII, Corporation Street.

At No. 10 was the White Swan. It had opened by 1818, when Thomas Weston was listed as licensee in the trade directory, and closed almost 100 years later in 1907. At Bagot Street, which links Lancaster Street to Corporation Street, was the Royal Elephant at No. 17. It was an early nineteenth-century public house updated by J.S. Davis from his plans of November 1878, and perhaps annoyingly was closed down barely five years later for an Improvement Scheme. Across the road at 18 Bagot Street was the White Hart, an early nineteenth-century beerhouse. The house was totally reconstructed under the direction of architect William Henman's plans of 1 February 1890. Its license was surrendered under the 'fewer but better' scheme in 1937. The King's Arms at 83 surrendered its license in 1928. The pub had originated one hundred years earlier in 1825. Again of the same period was the Beehive, a beerhouse updated by Thomas Kemp's plans of 16 April 1880. There is no record of its closure.

Moland Street had two licensed premises; the Horse & Jockey, whose license was abandoned under the Improvement Scheme of 1883, that saw the start of Corporation Street, and the Bull's Head at 110, which opened in 1818 and closed in 1903, right at the tail end of the cutting of Corporation Street and the cutting of its continuation, Aston Road North. In Fisher Street, now lost beneath Aston University, was the Hope & Anchor, at No. 35. Joseph Ansell, founder of the brewery, was licensee here in the early 1850s. Having left, the pub was taken over by Holder's Brewery, but did eventually become an Ansell's house in the 1920s. The Hope & Anchor closed in 1939, the site being acquired for the construction of Aston Technical College, fore-runner of Aston University. The Dog & Pheasant, at 23 Fisher Street, was also a Holder's house. There by 1822, its license was surrendered under the Improvement Scheme of 1883.

The Queen's Head in Aston Street was in existence by 1750. *Aris's Gazette* records the sale of its lease in its March edition:

> To be Lett, and enter'd upon immediately The Queen's Head Inn, at the End of Lichfield Street, Birmingham, being where six ways meet, with good stabling, a good pit to water Horses, with all other necessary conveniences, and a Spot of Ground near adjoining for a Bowling-Green, if desired.

In 1767, Birmingham's first trade directory lists Mary Cash as licensee. There are no further entries for this substantial house, and it would appear that it became the Swan with Two Necks. This house is shown on William Westley's Plan of Birmingham for 1731, but is not named. Humphrey Bacon is the earliest known licensee of the Swan. His obituary occurs in the *Gazette* for 13 January 1800. He had been licensee from pre-1787. In 1852 the Swan was advertised as 'newly rebuilt'. In 1883, like other houses here, it was obliged to surrender its license for the continuing development of Corporation Street. The license was returned in the following year, and this house continued in business until July 1933, when it was closed and demolished for the building of the Central Fire Station.

At 8 Aston Street was the Saracen's Head, opened in 1864 under John Bancroft. There are no further directory entries after 1868. Across the road at 9 Aston Street was the Talbot, in existence by 1767. In November 1791 the house became the meeting place of a number of local men opposed to the intended building of a brass-house nearby. In the following century, 1854, the pub was renamed the Exhibition. Its licensee was John Levinson. In 1865 the house changed its name again, and became the Bull & Lion. John Hall was licensee. The house is now long gone. Nearby was the Golden Lion, formerly the White Lion, established pre-1791. At one time the Golden Lion was at 9 Aston Street too, the product of street renumbering.

WM. SHEPPARD & SONS,
OMNIBUS, CAB, & CAR PROPRIETORS

SWAN WITH TWO NECKS MEWS,
100, Aston Street, Birmingham;
AND KING'S HEATH, NEAR MOSELEY.

First-class Carriages for Weddings, in scarlet or blue liveries, with bay or grey Horses; Vehicles for Private and Pic-Nic Parties. Post Horses and Carriages let for hire.

J. F. & A. SHEPPARD, Proprietors.

A Victorian advertisement for the Swan with Two Necks.

George Thomas was licensee up to 1795. He was followed by William Richards, William Ford and William Lamb, taking the pub well into the following century. In the directory of 1854 there is reference to a further Golden Lion, in Golden Lion Passage, which ran alongside of the pub. Two licensees are given, so obviously there were two distinct licensed premises. By the following year things were back to normal with just the one licensee – for the Golden Lion. The two premises may just be a mistake on behalf of the compilers of the 1854 directory. This old house, apparently never updated by the likes of James & Lister Lea or William Jenkins, was closed in 1917 and demolished as part of a road-widening scheme. The site now lies beneath Aston University campus. The General Wolfe was a pleasant little early nineteenth-century house, whose first known licensee was Charles Ward, landlord from 1811 to 1825. The house survived the Improvement Schemes along Aston Street, and in 1934 was restyled at ground-floor level in a very pleasing mock-Tudor build, with herring-bone brick and leaded windows. The house fell victim to the expansion of the 24-acre Aston Science Park. Its last licensee was the eccentrically named Mr Kaljo Uussalu. At 32 Aston Street was the Lord Nelson, dating from 1854. The Dog was at No. 34 from 1820 to 1835, and the Board was at 38 from 1840 to 1865. They too are now gone beneath the campus.

The Warwick Castle at 48-49 Aston Street was opened in 1818 by George Earp. He was followed by John Mangold, listed in Pigot's Directory as 'John Marigold'. How easily a man's reputation is soiled by the slip of a pen. After Mangold came Mrs Mary Hawkesford *et al* until the pub's closure in 1899 as part of the Improvement Scheme and the completion of Corporation Street. The house was rebuilt, and opened later that year under Alfred Simcox. No doubt on a warm summer's day in the 1950s, the door propped open by a stool, the customers of the Warwick Castle would have glanced across the road to look at the construction of Aston Technical College, little realising that its metamorphosis into Aston University would see the old pub's demise in the creeping expansion of its campus. The Warwick Castle closed in 1976. The Old Peacock was at 55 Aston Street and was a substantial, three-storey early nineteenth-century public house that faced onto the then cobbled street scene of Gosta Green. It opened in 1818, eventually became an M&B house, and closed in 1937. The New Peacock, at 49, perversely opened ten years earlier in 1808, was taken over by Holder's Brewery, updated by architect William Wykes in March 1888, and was closed in 1963 for the development of the Gosta Green area.

The Swan with Two Necks, Gosta Green, 1830.

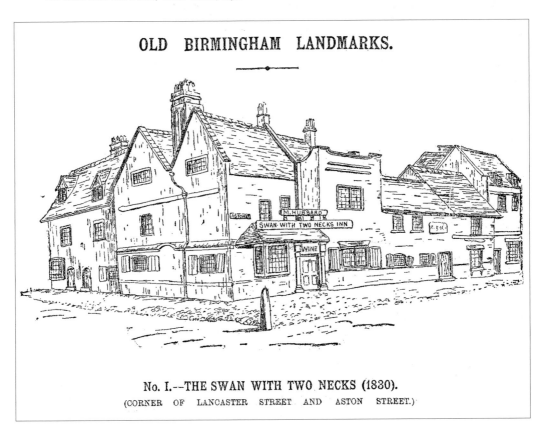

OLD BIRMINGHAM LANDMARKS.

No. I.--THE SWAN WITH TWO NECKS (1830).
(CORNER OF LANCASTER STREET AND ASTON STREET.)

The Grapes was a licensed victuallers at 81 Aston Street, dating from 1791 with Charles Taberner listed as landlord. By 1812 it had acquired an additional 'large capital, well-built and convenient malthouse'. Extensive alterations took place to the Grapes under the direction of architect E. Holmes, based on his plans of 24 November 1877. This house closed in the 1950s. There were a number of beerhouses along Aston Street that have come to light through oblique references. The Malt Shovel features in an advertisement in *Aris's Gazette* in 1770, as does the Seven Stars in 1767. The New Inn appears in the directory of 1797, and the Brown Lion comes to light with its rebuild from the plans of Charles J. Hodson (17 October 1877). Needless to say, they are all gone – as indeed are the Blue Anchor, on the corner of Aston Street and Sheep Street, dating from 1812 and closed in 1935, and the Dog & Duck at 40 Sheep Street, opened by 1823 and closed in 1911. The Coopers' Arms at 33 Potter Street, and the Dog at No. 50, both closed in 1883.

In Gosta Green itself there is now only one pub surviving, the Sacks of Potatoes. Originally a beerhouse, it opened in 1865 under licensee William Adams. It gained a full license in 1951. Then landlord, Francis George, purchased the full license from the Licensing Justices for £1,100. The pub was an M&B house, but is now free. At Lower Gosty Green, as it was then called, was the Cock, of 1767 under landlord William Bayes. Around the corner from the Sacks is Lister Street. At No. 13 was the Holte Arms, taking its name from the old family who built Aston Hall. Dating from 1827, the pub was later taken over by

Above: *The Sacks of Potatoes, Gosta Green.*

Opposite: *Advertisement, the Golden Lion, Gosta Green.*

the Holt Brewery (no relation), and closed in 1889. The brewery had taken its name from Holt Street, where it was situated. The Union Mill at 7 Holt Street took its name from the nearby steam-powered flour mill, and opened around 1800 under landlord Thomas Keeling. By 1829 the house was known as the Old Union Mill Inn. Taken over by Holt's, it later became an Ansell's house. The Pot of Beer, a late 1970s Ansell's house, was built in the old Holt Brewery, then known as Ansell's No. 2 Brewery. At 95 Holt Street was the Horse & Groom. It was in existence by 1818, with Lewis Jeeson as landlord, and closed less than a century later, in 1911. Charles Hill was the last licensee.

Heneage Street was named after Heneage Legge, a descendant of the Holte's of Aston Hall. In this street was the Eagle, a beerhouse dating from 1854 and the Rising Sun, another early nineteenth century beerhouse, which closed in 1957. The Bloomsbury Tavern was in existence by 1841, and closed in 1921. The Grapes at 179 Heneage Street, opened in 1859 and closed in 1956, and the Shepherd & Shepherdess dated from 1838. In 1956 its landlord was George Shimmelfening. The house closed in 1961. The whole street was then cleared away, and now lies beneath the university campus.

Woodcock Street pubs were either bird or beast. There was the Woodcock of 1828, under Irishman Robert O'Neil, the Roebuck which surrendered its beerhouse license in May 1909, the Stag & Pheasant, an M&B house at 24 Woodcock Street, demolished in 1931, the Hare & Hounds at 86, opened in 1818 and closed fifty years later, the Black Horse, a splendid

The Black Horse, Woodcock Street and Jennens Road.

high-Victorian public house on the corner of Jennens Road is still open for business. Its predecessor of the same name, on the same site, originated pre-1799. Non-animal in name here in Woodcock Street was the Gardeners Arms, a Holder's Brewery house closed in 1936. In Duke Street was the Red Cow; alterations to this beerhouse were carried out to the designs of architect W.N. Teague from his plans of 15 March 1882. The Red Lion at 72 Duke Street was another beerhouse not recorded by name in the directories until 1937. The Duke of York was popular with television people when the BBC had studios here. It was an old M&B house, reputedly 200 years old. It closed for the last time on New Year's Eve, 1973. Ironically the Duke was also popular with Aston University staff – ironically, because it was demolished for the expansion of the university. Aston University is responsible for more pubs disappearing than the war-time Blitz on Birmingham. Gem Street, remembered for its Industrial School, was originally known as New Thomas Street. The name changed in 1863. The Crown & Anchor opened around 1822 under landlord John Overton. It was forced to close for the insidious expansion of Aston University. On the next corner was Lawrence Street, with just one known licensed premise, the King William IV at No. 16. It was obliged to surrender its license in 1883. Prospect Row, just off Coleshill Street, had five pubs. The Castle Inn, at No. 5, was a nice old M&B house; built in red brick and terracotta in 1865, it closed a century later in 1965. The Bell was at 19 Prospect Row. Established by 1832, architects Fresno & Cheatle updated it in September 1896. The Bell became a City Brewery house, later taken over by Holder's then M&B. It closed in 1907 as part of Chamberlain's 'fewer but better' scheme in 1907. At 23 Prospect Row was the Bull's Head, an eighteenth-century house now gone beneath the campus. Also here was the Black Horse, pre-1806, and closed in 1838, and the oddly named Tollett's Stores, a beer and wine licensed premises, closed in 1915. At 16 Cross Street, just off Coleshill Street, but now gone, was the Red Lion, listed in the trade directory of 1767. John Harris was landlord. At 13 (Old) Cross Street was the Shepherd & Shepherdess, a pub dating from 1812. It was closed under the Improvement Scheme of 1887.

There was a plethora of pubs in Coleshill Street, the continuation of Dale End. At 11 Coleshill Street was the Horse & Groom, established by 1841, but closed by 1870. The Green Man at No. 36 was a late eighteenth-century public house which had closed by 1906. The Junction was at 39, and appears to have been a very short-lived pub. It opened in 1854 and closed in 1856. The Angel was a licensed victuallers at 63 Coleshill Street. There was a horse repository here in 1773, and regular horse sales were held in the pub yard. There is no evidence of the Angel being updated, and its license was called in under the 'fewer but better' scheme in 1915. The Black Lion was at 82 Coleshill Street. It was a mid-eighteenth-century house;

Holder's Rodney Inn, Coleshill Street, 1870s.

143

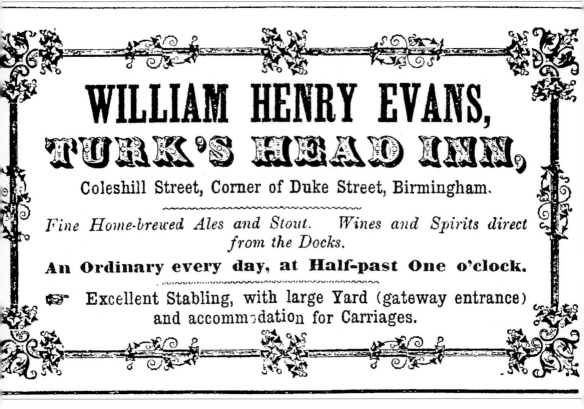

WILLIAM HENRY EVANS,
TURK'S HEAD INN,
Coleshill Street, Corner of Duke Street, Birmingham.

Fine Home-brewed Ales and Stout. Wines and Spirits direct from the Docks.

An Ordinary every day, at Half-past One o'clock.

☞ **Excellent Stabling, with large Yard (gateway entrance) and accommodation for Carriages.**

Advertisement, the Turk's Head, Coleshill Street.

William Griffith was landlord in 1767. The Black Lion closed in 1929 as part of the redevelopment scheme focused on Gosta Green and the construction of the Central Fire Station. The Prince of Wales at 85 opened in 1927. It was named after the man who later became Edward VIII. The house closed during the 1960s for the ever expanding Aston University campus.

The Rodney Inn at 89 Coleshill Street was a late Georgian house. Its most notable licensee was ex-butcher Henry Holder. His was a musical pub, with a large purpose-built entertainment hall, later expanded into Holder's Concert Hall. About 1885 the Rodney was pulled down and replaced by a post office. The Concert Hall later became the Gaiety Theatre. The Turk's Head at No. 59 was originally a home-brew house established on the corner of Duke Street. Thomas Yates was licensee from 1783 to 1817. The house was bought up by a company called Elson & Hilditch in 1868. It was modernised by architect William Wykes in 1881, and bombed by the Luftwaffe in 1940. It suffered a direct hit. Luckily no fatalities are listed. The Recruiting Sergeant was at 89 Coleshill Street from 1833 to 1839. The road was redeveloped and the street renumbered, giving No. 89 to the Rodney above.

At 102 Coleshill Street, on the corner with 1 (Old) Cross Street, was the Rising Sun. It was a Georgian house with so many add-ons over the years that it became a building full of strange ups and downs, in and outs and cosy corners, which gave it a distinctive character. A home-brew-house, it brewed a very potent beer called 'Rising Sunbeams', four pints of

·THE "RISING SUN," COLESHILL STREET.

The Rising Sun, Coleshill Street, c. 1870.

which were reckoned to be enough for any man. The house was a noted army recruiting house, the Union flag flying from its upper storey. The Rising Sun was updated by Edward Holmes in August 1880, and with slight modifications was the house that survived up to 1974. The Hope & Anchor was a licensed victuallers at 110 Coleshill Street. It originated in 1800 and remained open until 1915, when it was obliged to surrender its license. The Lichfield Tavern in Coleshill Street was run by Thomas Tabberner from 1797 until his death in March 1805. This house closed in 1835. Not so far away at 115 Coleshill Street was the Waggon & Horses, an early nineteenth-century house which closed in 1865.

Of the numerous beerhouses here, there was the Duke's Head of 1863 under J. Sims, the American Bar which lost its license in 1915, the Unicorn, dating to 1767 under Samuel Field, the Lamp of the same year under landlady Rebecca Hammond, the King Bruce, rebuilt from William Jenkins' plans of 18 August 1888, but closed in 1915, and the Peacock, another house dating from 1767, taken over by Holt's and later Ansell's, and now gone like many a good public house beneath the campus of Aston University.

The Jennens Estate

The Jennens estate, just off Dale End, was developed from the early eighteenth century. It was encompassed by Coleshill Street, Belmont Row, Curzon Street, Duddeston Row and Masshouse Lane. At 30-31 Masshouse Lane was the Coach & Horse, a home-brew house dating from 1865. It was taken over by the City Brewery Company of Lichfield. The house was updated by Richard McDaniel from his plans of December 1878. It closed pre-1900. At 20 Jennens Row was the Globe, a former beerhouse originating in 1861. The house gained a full license in 1956, when landlord Stanley Capewell paid the Licensing Justices the fee of £800. The Globe closed in 1966 as part of a post-Inner Ring Road redevelopment. Chapel Street, named after St Bartholomew's church, had a few pubs, including the delightfully named Mug House at No. 7. The name is a seventeenth-century term for an ale house. It was a late eighteenth-century house on the corner of Drury Lane, with a large coach entrance and yard off Drury Lane. In February 1803 it is named as Davis's Mug House, taking its name from a former licensee. The Mug House closed in 1896. At 26 was the George, dating from 1818 under licensee John Scarlett. It closed in 1865. The Crown & Anchor was at 30 Chapel Street. It was taken over by Allsopp & Sons, and updated by Birmingham architects Owen, Ward & Partners in 1896. This house surrendered its license to the Justices in 1915. The Coach & Horses at No. 15 dated from 1767, but had gone by 1780. The General Wolfe, a beerhouse, is named in the obituary of former owner Hugh Bolton, in March 1893. In Doe Street was the Duke of York, originating between 1812 and 1815, and closing in 1904.

Not too far away in Buck Street was the Sea Horse, one of Victorian Birmingham's classic pubs. It was situated on the corner of Fox's Court. In existence for nearly one hundred years, around 1878 it 'forsook its old respectability', as Bernard Porter related (*Birmingham Weekly Post*, 9 March 1912), 'and decking out its ground floor front in a garish fashion, it blossomed forth a gin palace. Lamps were made to project from a heavy and elaborate cornice, and on their glass sides were painted representations of some weird and monstrous creature popularly supposed to represent the features and figure of a sea horse.' The original Georgian tavern was noted for the remarkable flavour of its home-brewed ale, known as 'Digbeth Water'. The cellars of the Sea Horse, where the ale was brewed, consisted of four enormous store barrels, each with a capacity of about 1,000 gallons. The tap on the barrels was placed midway along the barrel, and as the beer was drawn off to this level, a fresh brew again filled the cask. In this way the ale always had a combination of mellow and new. Thomas Humphries, a former button maker, was landlord from 1780 until his death in November 1798. Under later licensee Francis Marrian, it became home to the Musical Society. It was only after his departure that the society moved to the Clarendon in Temple Street. Marrian himself took over the Dolphin, just down the road, dying there in 1846. The Sea Horse was offered for sale in 1891, with just six years remaining on its lease. The house was closed down and re-opened as a religious institution, the Birmingham Central Mission.

Leading off from Buck Street (now gone) is Nova Scotia Street. At No. 4 was the George Inn, a beerhouse, brought to light with the obituary of former licensee James Fisher, who died in June 1809. He was there from 1774. At No. 10 was the George & Dragon, dating from 1818, closed down in 1860. The Retail Brewer, a somewhat unique name, was a beerhouse in Buck Street that was closed by the Licensing Justices in 1915. The Don Cossack Inn had the alternative address of 2 Hick's Square. It dated from 1818 as the Cossack. It was later

An advertisement for the Don Cossack Inn, Hick's Square.

renamed the Don Cossack in 1855. Despite the Crimean War, the name was not changed to something more patriotic, and the house survived up to 1905.

Fox Street is a narrow little street not far from Millennium Point. It is a bit of a backwater, but in its time it supported three public houses – now all gone. The Anchor was a beerhouse, which featured in an advertisement of 1800, notifying the public that its landlord was moving to the Plume of Feathers in Whittall Street. The Fox was at 12 Fox Street, and dated from around 1740. It survived the years, finally closing in 1912 under the 'fewer but better' scheme. The Ship, later the Old Ship, was a pub dating from 1797. Its first landlord was Joseph Wilshaw. It too went under Chamberlain's scheme in 1908. The next road along is Grosvenor Street. There is one directory-recorded public house here, the Bell of 1767, with John Evans. In Howe Street was the King's Arms at No. 9, dating from around 1840 under licensee Thomas Craggs. It was taken over by M&B and updated at the end of the century, given a new ground-floor front, a new bar and a rear smoke room. The King's Arms closed in the 1970s. The Howe Street Wine Vaults opened in 1861and closed in 1875. The Flag at 20 Howe Street was open by 1836 and had a large number of licensees, especially for a free house. It closed in 1923.

The Cardigan Arms in Cardigan Street was a beerhouse that surrendered its license in 1914. The Victoria, another Victorian beerhouse, was closed in 1929. The Grand Junction, a nod towards the nearby Curzon Street Railway Station, was at 39 Cardigan Street. It originated around 1839, a year after the opening of the station., and closed a century later in 1937, Mrs Lilly Jordan was its last licensee. Penn Street, just off Curzon Street, still survives. On its corner with Gopsall Street is the newly opened Moby Dick's, formerly the Eagle & Ball, that came into being in 1850. Later bought up by M&B in the early twentieth century, it is now a Banks's house.

The Railway Tavern in Duddeston Row was the earliest of the railway-named pubs in Birmingham. It originated in 1834, two years after the Act to construct the London & Birmingham Railway was passed into law. The licensee was William Beech. Ironically the house closed in 1839 when the actual line was completed, and the land was required by the railway.

Moby Dicks, formerly the Eagle & Ball, Penn Street.

The Unicorn was at 47 Duddeston Row. It dated from 1820. In 1834 it was bought by Thomas Jones, who renamed it the Thatched House. This pub was closed in 1890 when its lease expired, and the site was redeveloped. The Golden Horse at 53 Duddeston Row was situated on the corner of Bartholomew Row. It was a mid-eighteenth-century public house. John Finchet is listed as licensee in 1767. Alterations were carried out to the house following plans submitted by architect J.H. Glover on 12 October 1878. The house appears in an advertisement in the *Birmingham Echo* for 11 October 1913:

> ARTHUR SCOTT, Golden Horse, Duddeston Row. Holders Ales, B.B., Bass and Guinness. Proprietary Wines, Spirits and Cigars. Well appointed bars and smoke room. Commodious club room free to good society. Attention and civility to all.

A Holder's house, it was later taken over by M&B. It closed in 1936, at the height of the Great Depression.

Curzon Street was named after the Hon. Penn Assheton Curzon, who married the niece of landowner Charles Jennens. The road is more popularly associated with the old Classical-designed railway station situated here. Pubwise there was the appropriately named Railway Hotel at 60-64 Curzon Street, opened in 1848, and updated by architect Joseph Henry Glover (26 November 1877). It was demolished in the 1950s, but resurrected in a new-build, and named the Old Railway. It became a popular musical venue, and helped launch the careers of Led Zeppelin, Ozzy Osbourne and the Steve Gibbons Band. Chris Barber and his jazz band also played at the Old Railway. In 2004 the pub was served notice of closure for the development of the £6 billion Eastside project. The Liverpool Arms, a beerhouse, was altered and updated from architect William A. Phipson's designs of 26 May 1877. It has now closed. O'Neill's Ale House and Kitchen was opened in Curzon Street by Mick O'Neill in January 1992. It soon came into confusing conflict with the Granville in Broad Street, which was renamed O'Neill's by owners Bass, who had started up a chain of Irish theme-pubs under that name. The problem was resolved when the Granville agreed to be known as O'Neill's on Broad Street.

At the back of Curzon Street Station is Banbury Street. Here at No. 39 was the Black Horse. It originated in 1840, soon after the cutting of the street. In 1892 licensee James Middleton Lones brought in James & Lister Lea to update it. The Black Horse closed in the summer of 1914. Albert Vernon Evans was its last licensee.

The eastern boundary of the city centre is defined by Dartmouth and Lawley Middle Ring Roads, eventually linking up again with Curzon Street and the completion of this survey of the city centre pubs and beerhouses. In the process of the creation of the Middleway, all of the pubs mentioned below for Dartmouth Street have now gone. The Dartmouth Arms was at 15 Dartmouth Street. Eli Peters opened the house in 1840. He was followed by his son, Edward, and so on, into the twentieth century, the landlords came and went. By the 1920s the address had changed slightly to 61 Dartmouth Street. It survived the wars and the redevelopments of the 1960s, but fell victim to the Middle Ring Road scheme in the following decade. At 34 was a little-known public house, the Hen & Chickens, first listed in the trade directory of 1835. It was taken over by Davenport's and was one of less than a handful of this brewery's pubs in the city centre. The Hen & Chickens closed for the Ring Road. The Crown & Anchor at 62 Dartmouth Street opened in 1869, with John Dare as landlord. The Old Green Man at 79 Darmouth Street predated it by some eighteen years, opening in 1851 under Thomas Dowse. It too fell victim to the Middle Ring Road. At 149 was the Lord Raglan, named after the Crimean War 'hero'. It opened in 1855 under licensee Robert Holliss. *The Times* newspaper's coverage of the war castigated Raglan and his senior officers for incompetence. Lastly the Malt Shovel, at 152 Dartmouth Street. It originated around 1848; Samuel Osborn was its first directory recorded licensee. The house had closed by 1858, and by 1975 all trace of it and the street itself had gone.

Lawley Street is now Lawley Middleway; at No. 47 was the Seven Stars. It originated in 1839 on the corner of Belmont Row, then on the edge of the Victorian town. William Mills was its first licensee. In 1883 the address changed slightly to 101-103 Lawley Street. This was the address it maintained until its closure in 1921. The Lion & Butcher, an odd name for a pub, was at 52 Lawley Street. It opened in 1867 with William Bird as its first licensee. This house was on the corner of Curzon Street. In 1888 architect William Wykes was brought in to update the pub. He submitted his plans on 26 February. The Lion & Butcher closed in 1911. The White Tower, now known as Moriarty's, after its landlady, is at 126 Lawley Street. It was built to replace an earlier pub of the same name. The earlier house was in existence by 1827, with John Jenkins as its landlord. Joseph Bedford was the last licensee of the old pub when it closed in 1931 and first licensee of the new M&B pub when it opened in 1932. The White Tower is perhaps the finest surviving example of an art deco pub in the city. Internally, though it has undergone some change over the years, traces still remain. It is a pub that should be locally listed by the Council at least, if not nationally listed. The Railway Tavern is first listed in the trade directory of 1869. It was then at 132 Lawley Street, with William Jones as licensee. There was some street renumbering in 1880, and the house became 174 Lawley Street.

The White Tower, Lawley Street.

Jones, licensee for seventeen years, retired in 1886, and the pub appears to have closed soon after, or at least it does not feature in the directories after this date. At 205 Lawley Street was the Viaduct, taking its name from the nearby railway viaduct. C.A. Collett drew-up plans for the extension of the pub on 18 March 1899, by which time it had become an Ansell's tied house. It is first recorded by name in the trade directory of 1937, when beerhouses were first listed by name. On the edge of the city centre was the Swan with Two Necks, at 213 Lawley Street. It dated from 1848. James Archer was its first recorded landlord. The house survived for a century or more before closing in 1960. It languished for a year before it was demolished. At 280 Lawley Street was the Village Tavern, a beerhouse dating from the Victorian era. It closed in 1939. The Midland Tavern, another Victorian beerhouse, survived until 1977, but was cleared away for the construction of the Middleway. The Jolly Boatman, from the same period, was obliged to surrender its license to the Licensing Justices in May 1909. Two public houses in Lawley Street appear to have closed in 1829; the Coachmakers Arms, run by Edward Booth, and the Bell, run by Joseph Taylor. The Bell in Prospect Row, that opened in the following year, may have been its successor.

The Whittington & Cat commemorates pantomime favourite Dick Whittington, thrice Lord Mayor of London, and his equally famous cat. A short advertisement for this Lawley Street pub appears in the November 1913 edition of the *Birmingham Echo*:

TED MARGETTS, WHITTINGTON & Cat, Lawley St. (Late White Hart, Buckingham Street), Showells Noted Ales, bottled stout, wines and spirits, mellowed by age. Bars, smoke and club rooms. Accommodation for clubs.

Art Deco doorway of the White Tower.

The Railway Tavern, Lawley Street, pen and wash, 1886.

This pub, and so many others listed in this perambulation, have gone. Hitler destroyed a few, but by far the biggest culprit was progress. Poor progress gets the blame for so many things, especially brewers' greed. The closure of so many locals is saddening, but what is worse is to see tied houses gutted, just so a few more customers can be packed in. The excuse now is that security is improved, when everyone knows that with only one bar you need fewer staff. More than walls are lost, so too is the character of a pub. Likewise to see the closure of such architectural gems as the Woodman in Easy Row is equally sad, especially in a road scheme that was forty years out of date before it was even constructed. Thirty years later great stretches of the Inner Ring Roads have been torn down, an acknowledgement that the scheme was a failure, which had condemned those areas beyond the concrete collar to urban decay. As to the replacements of those pubs torn down by such schemes, by and large their 1960s replacements are not memorable.

It is easy to get nostalgic about the past – everything then was better, some like to think. But this was not always so. The benevolent paternalism of the 'fewer but better' scheme of the late Victorians was by and large a positive thing. The worst excesses of drunkenness and petty crime were eradicated by the process. The large road houses of the 1920s and '30s, in the outer suburbs, are not to everyone's taste, but in their time they provided a focal point on the new council estates. Invariably there were also sporting and social clubs attached – darts, pigeons, gardening.

Perhaps the two best things that have happened in the recent past have been an end to the Puritanical control of the Licensing Justices, who often acted in excess of their intended powers; and the break-up of the tied house system by the Monopolies Commission. Old public houses came up for sale, new public houses have come into being. The daft notion that all old pubs are good, and all new pubs are bad, is given the lie by just two pubs in the city centre (though I am sure that there are other good examples), the Wellington in Bennett's Hill, and the Old Joint Stock in Temple Row. Today we experience a greater choice and no more so than in the pubs of central Birmingham.

INDEX

British Oak, William St. 118
British Queen, Lee Bank Rd. 99
Broad St. Tavern, Broad St. 115
Brookes Vaults, Jamaica Row 68
Brown Lion, Aston St. 140
Brown Lion, Horse Fair 94
Brunswick Hotel, Lancaster St. 135
Brushmakers Arms, Cheapside 58
Bull & Lion, Aston St. 137
Bull's Head, Bishopgate St. 118
Bull's Head, Bow St. 100
Bull's Head, Camp Hill 63
Bull's Head, Moland St. 137
Bull's Head, Prospect Row 142-3
Bull's Head, Staniforth St. 135
Bull's Head, Water St. 128
Bull's Head, Wharf St. 117
Bunch of Grapes, Henrietta St. 127
Burton Stores, Parade 126
Burton Stores, Sherlock St. 75
Calthorpe Arms, Bath Row 107
Cambridge Inn, Cambridge St. 125
Cannonball, Adderley St. 45
Cardigan Arms, Cardigan St. 147
Castle, Deritend High St. 30
Castle, Moseley St. 62
Castle & Ball, Bordesley High St. 34
Castle & Falcon, Digbeth High St. 15
Castle Inn, Prospect Row 142
Castle Tavern, Upper Trinity St. 47-8
Cauliflower Ear, Banbury St. 44
Challenge, Water St. 128
Chapel, Fleet St. 128
Cheltenham Arms, Sherlock St. 75
Chequers, Bell Barn Lane 99
Chequers, Brickiln St. 135
Chequers, Park St. 37
City Arms, Lancaster St. 134
City Tavern, Bishopgate St. 118
Cleary's, Cheapside 58
Clement Arms, Gooch St. 87
Clement Arms, Upper Trinity St. 48
Clements Vaults, Digbeth High St. 15
Coach & Horses, Bordesley High St. 32

Coach & Horses, Chapel St. 146
Coach & Horses, Irving St. 99
Coach & Horses, Sherlock St. 74-5
Coach & Horses, Masshouse Lane 146
Coach & Horses, Upper Dean St. 68
Coach & Horses, Water St. 128
Coachmakers Arms, Lawley St. 150
Coachsmith's Arms, Watery Lane 48
Cock, Lower Gosty Green 140
Colmore Arms, Grosvenor St. West 119
Colmore Arms, Latimer St. 99
Colwyn, Gt. Colmore St. 99
Compasses, Alcester St. 59
Compasses, Broad St. 112
Compasses, Deritend High St. 29
Compasses, Inge St. 84, 86
Coopers Arms, Potter St. 140
Cottage of Content, Sheepcote St. 119
Craven Arms, Upper Gough St. 106
Crescent Tavern, Crescent 124
Criterion, Digbeth High St. 22
Criterion, Hurst St. 80
Criterion Vaults, Jamaica Row 68
Cross Guns, Lancaster St. 135
Cross Keys, Hurst St. 83-4
Cross Keys, Jamaica Row 68
Crown, Broad St. 112, 115
Crown, Oxford St. 38
Crown & Anchor, Chapel St. 146
Crown & Anchor, Dartmouth St. 149
Crown & Anchor, Gem St. 142
Crown & Anchor, Sherlock St. 74
Crown & Anchor, Watery Lane 48
Crown & Ball, Digbeth High St. 24
Crown & Barrel, Tennant St. 118
Crow's Nest, Inge St. 86
Crusader, Islington Row 118
Cup, Ruston St. 119
Daniel Lambert, Moseley St 61
Dartmouth Arms, Dartmouth St. 149
Davis' Mug House, Chapel St. 146

Death of General Wolfe, Digbeth High St. 24
Dog, Alcester St. 58-9
Dog, Aston St. 138
Dog, St. Martin's St. 118
Dog & Duck, Birchall St. 58
Dog & Duck, Holloway Head 100
Dog & Duck, Sheep St. 140
Dog & Partridge, Alcester St. 59
Dog & Partridge, Ellis St. 105
Dog & Partridge, Lee Bank Rd. 99
Dog & Partridge, Moseley St. 60
Dog & Pheasant, Fisher St. 137
Dolphin, Bromsgrove St. 72
Dolphin, Buck St. 146
Dolphin, Coventry St. 46
Dolphin, Irving St. 99
Don Cossack Inn, Hick Square 146-7
Drovers Arms, Moat Row 50
Dubliner, Digbeth High St. 15, 17
Duke of Cumberland, Freeman St. 36
Duke of Edinburgh, Birchall St. 58
Duke of Marlborough, Mount St. 126
Duke of Wellington, Communication Row 108
Duke of Wellington, Gooch St. 87
Duke of York, Doe St. 146
Duke of York, Duke St. 142
Duke of York, Holloway Head, 105
Duke of York, Horse Fair 90
Duke's Head, Coleshill St. 145
Dun Cow, Horse Fair 94
Eagle, Heneage St. 141
Eagle, Oozells St. North 120
Eagle & Ball, Ladywood Lane 119
Eagle & Ball, Moseley St. 60
Eagle & Ball, Penn St. 147
Eagle & Tun, Banbury St. 44
Earl Grey, Wrentham St. 77
Edgbaston Hotel, Lee Bank Rd. 99
Edgbaston Inn, Lee Bank Rd. 99
Elephant & Castle, Holliday St. 108
Exchange, Granville St. 117
Exhibition, Aston St. 137
Exhibition, King Edward's Place 121

Other local titles published by Tempus

Central Birmingham Pubs Volume I
JOSEPH MCKENNA

This fascinating volume records the pubs, inns, taverns and beerhouses of the central city, an area now within the present Inner Ring Road and the Bull Ring. This is the very heart of the city and although it comprises only one square mile and can be crossed by foot in less than half an hour, it is an area that has seen over 760 pubs – all of which are faithfully recorded here.

0-7524-3873-5

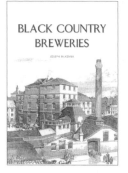

Black Country Breweries
JOSEPH MCKENNA

The Black Country was the industrial heartland of England, a harsh environment of coal and iron mines, of nail and chain making. Its people worked hard, and drank hard. This is the story of brewing in the region, from small scale home-brew houses to big brewers such as Mitchells and Butlers at Cape Hill and Banks' at Wolverhampton. Complete with over 100 illustrations this book provides a fascinating insight into the history of brewing in the Black Country.

0-7524-3722-4

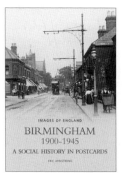

Birmingham 1900-1945: A Social History in Postcards
ERIC ARMSTRONG

This fascinating collection of over 200 archive postcards provides a nostalgic insight into the changing history of Birmingham over the period 1900-1945. For over a quarter of this time Britain was at war and the political and social changes felt were immense, not least in Birmingham, a major industrial city. This book will awaken memories of a bygone time for all those who worked or lived in this vibrant community.

0-7524-4037-3

Haunted Birmingham
ARTHUR SMITH AND RACHEL BANNISTER

From creepy accounts of the city centre to phantoms of the theatre, haunted pubs and hospitals, *Haunted Birmingham* contains a chilling range of ghostly phenomena. Drawing on historical and contemporary sources, you will hear about the landlady who haunts the site of her death, the two workmen who dies during the building of the Town Hall, the late Mayor who still watches over the city, the last man to be publicly hanged in Birmingham, and many more ghostly goings on.

0-7524-4017-9

If you are interested in purchasing other books published by Tempus, or in case you have difficulty finding any Tempus books in your local bookshop, you can also place orders directly through our website

www.tempus-publishing.com